Presented to Purchase College
by
Gary Waller, PhD Cambridge

State University of New York
Distinguished Professor

Professor
of Literature & Cultural
Studies, and Theatre &
Performance, 1995-2019
Provost 1995-2004

SHAKESPEARE AND SOCIETY

Shakespeare and Society

CRITICAL STUDIES IN
SHAKESPEAREAN DRAMA

By

Terence Eagleton

SCHOCKEN BOOKS · NEW YORK

Manufactured in the United States of America

For
RAYMOND WILLIAMS

Acknowledgements

I WOULD like to acknowledge my debt to several people who have influenced or helped with this book: to Dr R. D. Laing, whose work I had not discovered until many of the ideas here were formed, but whose insights have given me great help; to my wife, whose response to the book during the process of writing was my most valuable criticism; to Charles Swann, for his consistent help, interest and criticism in the final stages of writing. My chief debt, however, is to Raymond Williams, to whom I offer this as an extension of his own explorations, and without whose friendship and influence the book would not have been written.

All quotations from Shakespeare are taken from *The Complete Works*, ed. Peter Alexander (Collins, 1951).

T. E.

Contents

Introduction

THE studies of some of Shakespeare's problem plays, tragedies and Last Comedies in this book try to follow through certain themes in Shakespeare's work, and in doing so make up a whole way of looking at Shakespeare which seems to me particularly relevant to our own time. I have not tried to make an exhaustive study of a large number of plays, and there are some obvious omissions; but I have confined myself instead to a small group of plays which seem especially relevant to the ideas I am exploring.

I end, in a Conclusion, with a brief account of how the problems I have looked at in Shakespeare continue, in different terms but with essentially the same meanings, through the nineteenth century into our own time. In this way the Conclusion is meant to make explicit a sense of contemporary significance which I hope is there throughout the book: it is intended, not simply as a note on our own society, but as a description of the experience which shapes the way we look at Shakespeare. The problems which Shakespeare confronts are in some ways very much the problems which concern us, and we cannot examine these problems as they are present in his plays except through the focus of our own experience, as we cannot fully understand our own experience except through an understanding of Shakespeare. What we judge in the plays as relevant, what we actually see, is shaped by what we see in our own culture, in ourselves. For this reason I have used a vocabulary in discussing Shakespeare which may seem self-consciously modern: 'authentic', 'spontaneous', 'reciprocal' probably recur too often as critical terms, but this kind of language seems to me the way we can get closest to Shakespeare's ideas and feelings. I hope that the terms will justify themselves, if the book is read as a whole.

This study of Shakespeare can be described generally as a consideration of individual and society in the plays, but this is clearly too vague a formula to stand by itself without close analysis. A work proposing to discuss this kind of relationship needs to be above all a work of practical criticism, where the general assertion can be sustained by actual reference. But the study is offered, not only as an extension of our understanding of Shakespeare but as an extension of our understanding of person and society. In our own period we have come to discover new possibilities of relationship between individual and society which have caused us to re-think our descriptions of both terms; we are learning to feel beyond the abstract opposition of personal and social experience, and see this for what it is, as literally an abstraction. The converging experience of a number of thinkers, in culture and psychology, politics and philosophy, has given us definitions of person and society which make any straight division between individual life, and the social forms within which this is available, unthinkable. There is a particular difficulty in the fact that our understanding of this truth has developed within a sense that our society, in actuality, is stunting and distorting personal, spontaneous life, and that tension between the two is therefore vital. What must be avoided, in maintaining this essential tension, is the habit of seeing society as inevitably external, a repressive mechanism which *by definition* threatens individual authenticity. The effort to go beyond this deadlock, to see how the qualities of spontaneous life now available to us can be translated without loss into the terms of a whole culture, demands a new way of looking at both individual and society, a new kind of synthesis. It is a synthesis which is always liable to breakdown, into a merely personal affirmation, or a merely institutional concern; but the effort to make and sustain it is a natural consequence of our understanding that individual experience is no more merely private than society is merely public.

Our own sense of this problem comes directly from our experience of industrial society: this is the context within which we think, and in which the problems have to be solved. But our own experience has now reached a point where I believe we are able to understand Shakespeare in ways not possible before, and where this understanding is simultaneously an insight into our own condition. In this book I try to show the tension in some of Shakespeare's plays between the self as it seems to a man in its personal depth, and as it seems in action, to others, as part of and responsible to a whole society. Shakespeare lives the experience, both of breakdown and of healing, in an intense form: the effort to reconcile spontaneous life and social responsibility is, with him, a persistent concern. It is not a matter of learning from Shakespeare in any simple way: our formulation of the problem is not his, and our experience of it is therefore different. But to understand his attempts to grapple with the difficulties is inevitably to deepen our own understanding, and to recognise new ways forward.

CHAPTER ONE

Troilus and Cressida

I N Act III Scene 3 of *Troilus and Cressida*, Ulysses tries to jolt Achilles into action by pointing out that there is no such thing as private experience:

> . . . no man is the lord of anything,
> Though in and of him there be much consisting,
> Till he communicate his parts to others;
> Nor doth he of himself know them for aught
> Till he behold them formed in th'applause
> Where th'are extended . . .

Ulysses is not merely arguing that uncommunicated qualities are inferior or useless; the first three lines of the quotation could be taken as meaning this, and then the argument would be no more than the familiar point that man is a 'sociable' being, at his best when in relationship with others. But the real force of that 'lord of anything' comes through in the next lines, where Ulysses is saying that uncommunicated qualities don't have any real existence at all; a man is not simply known to others through communication, he can only know his own experience by putting it in a communicable form. He does not know his own reality as an individual and then communicate it: the reality forms in the communication. The kind of separation between himself and society which Achilles is trying to force is therefore serious: a man who contracts out of public life is contracting out of reality; he is dead. Individual identity is a public creation: a man is what his society makes of him; he has no meaning outside its response. It is, in fact, impossible to stand completely outside society, to disengage totally; the disengagement itself will usually be just another symptom of the society, part of its whole reality, as the cynicism of Achilles and Thersites is part of the general sickness they analyse and attack.

Troilus and Cressida suggests again and again that reality is a public process, a common creation, and the play seems to confirm Ulysses's view in its own techniques. This is evident particularly in the way that individuals come to be known through the descriptions of others: in the first scene of the play Pandarus describes Cressida's qualities to Troilus, and Troilus exclaims:

> . . . I tell thee I am mad
> In Cressid's love. Thou answer'st 'She is fair'—
> Pourest in the open ulcer of my heart—
> Her eyes, her hair, her cheek, her gait, her voice,
> *Handlest* in thy discourse . . .

The physical effect of 'handlest' is significant: it begins the suggestion, expanded throughout the play, that describing someone to someone else is more than a second-hand process, it is a way of actually mediating and conveying their reality to another, re-creating them as individuals. Cressida's reality, for Troilus, is at first totally in the possession of Pandarus: 'I cannot come to Cressid but by Pandar'. In the next scene, Pandarus reverses the process by describing Troilus to Cressida. Achilles re-creates the other Greeks by enact-

ing them to Patroclus; Ulysses speaks of Aeneas 'translating' Troilus to him (IV, 5); Agamemnon refuses to
be answered 'in second voice' when confronting Achilles
(II, 3). The image of the merchant, the mediator, the
go-between dominates the play, most obviously in
Pandarus, but also in the plotting of Ulysses to set Ajax
on to duel with Hector: two individuals are brought
together through and in terms of a third. Ulysses's
remark to Nestor when he first conceives the idea of
choosing Ajax to face Hector is significant of this
process:

> I have a young conception in my brain;
> Be you my time to bring it to some shape.   (I, 3)

Nestor will mediate Ulysses's own idea to him, he will
be the element through which the idea becomes real.
Two people can create, reciprocally, a reality: in the
relationships of Troilus and Cressida, Nestor and Ulysses, Achilles and Patroclus, a whole version of experience is created and sustained, and objective experience
can come, somehow, to exist in terms of this relationship.
Achilles and Patroclus create their own versions of the
other Greeks in a way which shapes the Greeks' actual
behaviour:

> And in the imitation of these twain—
> Who, as Ulysses says, opinion crowns
> With an imperial voice—many are infect.   (I, 3)

Objective reality is moulded to the distortions of the
personal version: Achilles imitates the Greeks, who in
turn imitate his imitations. In a similar way the reality
of Troy as an unconquered city takes its being, not
from itself, but from the inactivity of the Greeks:

. . . To end a tale of length,
Troy in our weakness stands, not in her strength.   (I, 3)

People, things, events can have their being 'in' other
realities, other contexts, existing only in terms of these.

Reality, according to Ulysses, is a common creation,
and because of this it is relative: it is the shared possession of a group of men, and can change as they change.
It is relative, too, because a number of different versions of reality may co-exist, each thinking itself the
centre. This is most evident in Troilus and Cressida
themselves. Their love is a new creation, the forging
of a permanent, autonomous reality: they make a
'bargain', a mutual commitment verified by and in
Pandarus:

Go to, a bargain made; seal it, seal it; I'll be the witness. Here
I hold your hand; here my cousin's. If ever you prove false one
to another, since I have taken such pains to bring you together,
let all pitiful goers-between be call'd to the world's end after my
name—call them all Pandars; let all constant men be Troiluses,
all false women Cressids, and all brokers between Pandars. Say
'Amen'.   (III, 2)

They see themselves, now, in terms of each other: they
find their real, authentic selves in the new reality of the
love-relationship:

I have a kind of self resides with you;
But an unkind self, that it self will leave
To be another's fool . . .   (III, 2)

Love makes a new self by fusing the two individuals,
and so to leave each other is to leave themselves, to
desert their authenticity. This is why Troilus, confronted with Cressida's unfaithfulness, reacts by seeing
her as two people: 'This is, and is not, Cressid'.

Cressida to him is the Cressida of their relationship; she has no meaning or existence for him outside this context, as Achilles, according to Ulysses, has no existence outside the defining judgements of his society. People and things seem to draw their meanings from their contexts, but because there are many different contexts, all liable to change, there can be continual confusion about 'real' meanings and values. Cressida, before her defection, thinks of her love for Troilus as standing at the centre of reality:

> . . . the strong base and building of my love
> Is as the very centre of the earth,
> Drawing all things to it.   (IV, 2)

and Achilles also sees himself as a centre: he

> . . . never suffers matter of the world
> Enter his thoughts, save such as doth revolve
> And ruminate himself. . .   (II, 3)

Ajax, also, is a centre, although a created one. Personal reality, according to Ulysses, is the property of the whole community, but reciprocally the whole common reality can become focused in one individual, who then exists in terms of it, as its pivot. Ajax is selected by the Greeks to represent them to the Trojans:

> It is suppos'd
> He that meets Hector issues from our choice;
> And choice, being mutual act of all our souls,
> Makes merit her election, and doth boil,
> As 'twere from forth us all, a man distill'd
> Out of our virtues; who miscarrying,
> What heart receives from hence a conquering part,
> To steel a strong opinion to themselves?   (I, 3)

Ajax, as the Greeks' representative, is supposed to be created out of their shared decision, 'distilled' from their pooled ideas and opinions; their cause will be entirely in his keeping, and will stand or fall by his personal action. The reflexive movement is clear again, as it was with the imitations of Achilles: Ajax is a created agent whose actions will in turn mould the fortunes of his creators. He will be the element to mediate them, as a community, to the Trojans: they will 'dress him up in voices', make him the living embodiment of their cause, defined and controlled by them. Indeed Ajax, as a man, is described by Alexander to Cressida as an amalgam of other people's qualities, a bundle of scraps:

This man, lady, hath robb'd many beasts of their particular additions: he is as valiant as the lion, churlish as the bear, slow as the elephant . . . There is no man hath a virtue that he hath not a glimpse of, nor any man an attaint but he carries some stain of it . . . he hath the joints of everything; but everything so out of joint that he is a gouty Briareus, many hands and no use . . . (I, 2)

Nestor's comment on Ulysses's plan to set Ajax on to Hector and thus stir Achilles into life brings home again the idea of a reciprocally created reality:

Two curs shall tame each other: pride alone
Must tarre the mastiffs on, as 'twere their bone.   (I, 3)

Pride is the common element through which Ajax and Achilles can be played off against each other.

Helen, for the Trojans, is also a commonly created reality, the centre of a whole world-view. She exists for them only in terms of this: their discussion of her in Act II Scene 2 is in fact a discussion of the war she symbolises. She is the pivot of a quarrel in which the individual honours of the Trojans are tied up, and in talking about her they are talking about themselves. They define themselves, individually, in terms of the self-expressive action which the war she symbolises affords them, and their self-definition, their sense of personal meaning and identity, is thus in and through her. She represents a quarrel

> Which hath our several honours all engag'd
> To make it gracious.

as Troilus says, and Hector declares that keeping Helen is

> . . . a cause that hath no mean dependence
> Upon our joint and several dignities.   (II, 2)

Helen thus serves the same purpose for the Trojans as Ajax serves for the Greeks: she mediates their own sense of themselves to them, she is their living reflection, the arch which Ulysses describes to Achilles as reverberating back the human voice, or the gate of steel which 'receives and renders back' the sun's heat. She ceases to exist for the Trojans as a person and becomes merely a point of reference for their individual self-expression, lending them a tenuous unity. The evident difference between the idealised Helen of Troilus's speeches and the flirt we see on stage is intended to underline the danger involved in this kind of seeing. It is not only the danger involved in the damage done to Helen as a person, the fact that she, like Ajax, is reduced to a pawn while being idealised as a pivot, implicitly compared, by Troilus, to merchandise; it is the danger involved in the fact that a created meaning may be quite different from an actual meaning —

the process of reality-making may be completely at odds with things as they really are.

The same problem is there with the Greeks. If it is true, as Ulysses says, that we know ourselves only in terms of each other, then intrinsic meanings and values seem to be cancelled; a man is the sum-total of his relationships, and his reality as a person is flexible, it may alter as the whole pattern of relationships alters. The fact that personal identity is involved with the whole process of communication which is society can be seen as positive: it leaves no room for the individualism of Troilus, affirming the need for personal action to be responsible, responsive to the estimates of a whole society. But it can lead, also, to bewildering relativism, as Thersites's baiting of Achilles and Patroclus makes clear:

ACHILLES ... Come, what's Agamemnon?

THERSITES Thy commander, Achilles. Then tell me, Patroclus, what's Achilles?

PATROCLUS Thy Lord, Thersites. Then tell me, I pray thee, what's Thersites?

THERSITES Thy knower, Patroclus. Then tell me, Patroclus, what art thou?

PATROCLUS Thou must tell that knowest.   (II, 3)

Men, as individuals, are defined and known in terms of their relationships with each other, in constant reciprocity: they possess each other's realities, and Patroclus must ask Thersites about his own identity. Thersites brings the process of reciprocal definition artificially to an end by defining himself in relation to Patroclus rather than to someone else, thus making Patroclus knowable in terms of himself. But in fact the process could go on indefinitely, since Thersites's conception of Patroclus includes his conception of how other people see Patroclus, and how Patroclus sees himself (which again depends on how other people see him). What this brief tracing of the process indicates is that the reality of any one member of the Greek camp can only be described in terms of the realities of all the others, and since all the realities include one another, the process is circular, as Patroclus's clinching remark suggests. The system is enclosed, but it can be traced round indefinitely. Patroclus can only know himself in terms of Thersites ('Thou must tell me that knowest'), but Thersites's own sense of himself is part of a process which includes Patroclus: the answer to the question 'what are you?' for Thersites would have to describe the whole nexus of relationships which includes Patroclus. In fact, Thersites tries to set himself outside the system, to detach himself by defining himself in terms of knowing someone else rather than being known: by doing this he can seem to take an absolute stand. But the dominant feeling of the interchange is the feeling of circularity, the circularity of Ulysses's reverberating arch; society is a continuous and changing inter-definition, and no self, no meaning or value or action, is fixed.

Achilles fails to realise this. In continuing to define himself by past action, he misses the point, made by Ulysses, that identity is existential, relative to an actual context. Past achievements are husks, dead selves: the self must be constantly fluid, achieving and advancing, responsive only to the present. The scraps which Time consumes

> . . . are good deeds past, which are devour'd
> As fast as they are made, forgot as soon
> As done. Perseverance, dear my Lord,
> Keeps honour bright. To have done is to hang
> Quite out of fashion, like a rusty mail
> In monumental mock'ry.   (III, 3)

Men do not have intrinsic identities: selves are conferred on them by the common process of creation in which they share, and they make others as they themselves are made. But what if everyone is deluded over a particular matter? The point is made, incidentally, by Thersites, railing against Patroclus:

> Let thy blood be thy direction till thy death. Then if she that lays thee out says thou art a fair corse, I'll be sworn and sworn upon't she never shrouded any but lazars.   (II, 3)

To a woman who had only seen lepers an ugly man might seem handsome: Thersites's comment voices Shakespeare's uneasiness about this kind of valuation. Things, surely, are sometimes as they are, in spite of the human meanings put on them, the versions of reality into which they are drawn. The feeling is there early in the play, when Pandarus, after trying to describe Cressida to Troilus in an attractive way, gives up irritably:

> Faith, I'll not meddle in it. Let her be as she is: if she be fair, 'tis the better for her; an she be not, she has the mends in her own hands.   (I, 1)

In the next scene, Pandarus and Cressida begin to argue about the relative merits of Troilus and Hector and come to agree that comparison is impossible:

PANDARUS Well, I say Troilus is Troilus.

CRESSIDA Then you say as I say, for I am sure he is not Hector.

PANDARUS No, nor Hector is not Troilus in some degrees.

CRESSIDA 'Tis just to each of them: he is himself.

Both agree that both men are as they are: but a minute later they are arguing about shades of brown, and Cressida's caustic reply to Pandarus's compromising 'brown and not brown' is 'To say the truth, true and not true' —she rejects his nice distinctions for the feeling that there must be some fixed truth in the matter. But the rejection of comparison is both a rejection of relativism and a rejection of *reason*: reason, throughout the play, is presented in terms of weighing scruples and making subtle distinctions, and it operates by bringing things into relation with each other, which is what comparison does also. Reason itself is involved with relativism, and a rejection of the latter may mean a rejection of the former: the appeal to things as they are in themselves, independently of context and relation, leaves one simply with brute realities with which nothing can be done. A minor point at the end of this scene brings this out strongly: Aeneas asks Troilus 'Wherefore not afield?' to which Troilus replies 'Because not there'. The rejection of explanation and context implied in this answer is an appeal to things as they are, brute fact, which is quite sterile.

Reality as humanly created, then, is dangerous; reality seen as things-in-themselves can be sterile. A half-rejection of reality as a common, flexible creation is there in the very speech, that of Ulysses to Achilles, which advances the idea most powerfully. Ulysses begins, as we have seen, by emphasising the public nature of identity: a man is the sum total of his actions, he is as he reveals himself in the public world. But to underline the importance of a man's public reputation, Ulysses points to the way that Ajax will be renowned for fighting Hector, in spite of his evident stupidity:

> Heavens, what a man is there!
> A very horse that has he knows not what!
> Nature, what things there are
> Most abject in regard and dear in use!
> What things again most dear in the esteem
> And poor in worth!   (III, 3).

In pointing to the difference between Ajax's intrinsic merit and the public reputation he will gain, Ulysses has almost given away his case: he sets out to prove that men are only what they are in the public eye, and then, to stress the importance of that eye, shows how it can make an intrinsically worthless man into something valuable. But by this appeal to 'Nature', to a fixed order of intrinsic values, Ulysses has denied the force of the original case. He is trying to use a point which should in fact go against the public creation of value – the fact that it can make a worthless man appear valuable – into a point in its favour, by presenting it as an instance of the power of this public image-making.

But the real weakness of Ulysses's viewpoint comes out in the attitude of the Trojans. The quarrel between Troilus and Hector over whether to continue the war or to release Helen is a quarrel between two totally opposed ways of seeing. Hector believes that an issue must be decided by a rational weighing of the elements involved, and that only then can action take place;

he believes in permanent values accessible to reason. Troilus believes that value is a human creation, humanly conferred; things have value in so far as an intensity of human activity gives them it, and value is thus something which grows within the process of activity, as the Greeks' identities grow within the process of action. The conflict is a direct one, between an essentialist and an existentialist vision:

HECTOR Brother, she is not worth what she doth cost
  The keeping.

TROILUS What's aught but as 'tis valued?

HECTOR But value dwells not in particular will:
  It holds his estimate and dignity
  As well wherein 'tis precious of itself
  As in the prizer. 'Tis mad idolatry
  To make the service greater than the god;
  And the will dotes that is attributive
  To what infectiously itself affects,
  Without some image of th'affected merit.   (II, 2)

Hector sees value as an amalgam of the intrinsic worth of a thing, and the actual worth it derives from its context, in relation to a particular prizer. To disregard intrinsic value leads to insane disproportion— it is 'to make the service greater than the god', to force an incongruity between the degree of energy expended on a thing and its objective worth. In this way of looking, human energy and activity become everything, and rational purpose and function nothing; objective reality becomes grist to the mill of personal activity, as the Greeks, for Achilles, are simply food for private satire, and the war, for the Trojans, is a means to self-definition in action. Moreover, if value lies in human energy, in the human response, what becomes important is not the end of activity, but activity itself; acting becomes a value in itself, and it is the process, not the achievement, which matters. Action confers value on itself, in a circular process, as the image of a will being attributive to 'what infectiously itself affects' suggests.

This is evident in Troilus's attitude to Helen:

> Is she worth keeping? Why, she is a pearl
> Whose price hath launch'd above a thousand ships,
> And turn'd crown'd kings to merchants.   (II, 2)

His argument is a *non sequitur*: he appeals, when asked to prove Helen's value, to all the activity which she has caused, but of course the activity can only be justified by proving *first* that Helen is valuable, as Hector wishes to do. The process is circular, as the Greeks' inter-definition is circular: Troilus makes Helen valuable by fighting for her, and she then assumes a value which justifies his continued fighting.

The Greeks create each other's identities, the Trojans create their own values, and in both cases the process is circular and self-sustaining: there is no appeal outside the existential context of human action to an absolute norm, the process can appeal only to itself for justification. The rhythm of circularity dominates the play: activity is seen constantly as self-consuming. Ulysses sees uncontrolled appetite like this in his famous speech on degree:

> Then everything includes itself in power,
> Power into will, will into appetite;
> And appetite, an universal wolf,
> So doubly seconded with will and power,
> Must make perforce an universal prey,
> And last eat up himself.   (I, 3)

Appetite consumes power and will (which have con-
sumed everything else), and strengthened by these can
more quickly consume everything and itself: the process is circular, but it is also a continual telescoping, a
continual increase of bulk and power which drives the
circle on at a faster rate. As with Hamlet's mother,
increase of appetite grows from what it feeds on.

Self-praise without reference to the judgements of
others is another example of circularity: Aeneas reminds
himself that

> The worthiness of praise distains his worth,
> If that the prais'd himself bring the praise forth . . . (I, 3)

and Agamemnon's description of pride to Achilles
makes this clearer:

> He that is proud eats up himself. Pride is his own glass,
> his own trumpet, his own chronicle; and whatever praises
> itself but in the deed devours the deed in the praise.   (II, 3)

Praise without deed is self-devouring because it is an
evaluation closed to the judgement of others: only
through action, public self-disclosure, can self-judge-
ment be verified and sealed. Achilles's pride is self-
conferred value, without regard either to intrinsic merit
or the conferred merit of others: in this condition,
objective values and proportions are lost as surely as
they are in Troilus's private conferment of value:

> Things small as nothing, for request's sake only,
> He makes important; possess'd he is with greatness,
> And speaks not to himself but with a pride
> That quarrels at self-breath. Imagin'd worth
> Holds in his blood such swol'n and hot discourse

That 'twixt his mental and his active parts
Kingdom'd Achilles in commotion rages,
And batters down himself. (II, 3)

Love seems to involve the same circularity, as Paris's remark to Helen suggests:

He eats nothing but doves, love; and that breeds hot blood, and hot blood begets hot thoughts, and hot thoughts beget hot deeds, and hot deeds is love. (III, 1)

Lechery, as Thersites says, 'eats itself': like Troilus's idea of action, it sustains itself by its own energies, without outside reference, and, like the action of time in Ulysses's speech (III, 3), it is constantly devouring and overriding its own brief achievements:

Th'expense of spirit in a waste of shame
Is lust in action; and, till action, lust
Is perjur'd, murd'rous, bloody, full of blame . . .
Mad in pursuit, and in possession so;
Had, having, and in quest to have, extreme;
A bliss in proof, and prov'd, a very woe;
Before, a joy propos'd; behind, a dream . . .   (Sonnet 129)

The circularity is there as an echo in minor images: Troy's towers, Ulysses says, 'must kiss their own feet' (IV, 5); Patroclus declares that 'those wounds heal ill that men do give themselves' (III, 3). Circularity comes from conferred value: self-conferred value as with Achilles, individually conferred value as with Troilus, mutually conferred value as with the Greeks. In all three cases, the permanent, intrinsic values which Ulysses can advance as a theoretical framework for action (I, 3) are cancelled.

But intrinsic values seem no more helpful as a guide

to action. The dissension in the Greek camp shows the failure of rational weighing and evaluating as a motive to action: the Greeks' rationality devours itself as surely as does the Trojans' activity. Reason obstructs itself: the very closeness and complexity of its functioning becomes a barrier to the action it is meant to motivate. The obstruction is felt as a radical flaw in the nature of action itself:

> The ample proposition that hope makes
> In all designs begun on earth below
> Fails in the promis'd largeness; checks and disasters
> Grow in the veins of actions highest rear'd,
> As knots, by the conflux of meeting sap,
> Infects the sound pine, and diverts his grain
> Tortive and errant from his course of growth.   (I, 3)

Reason is necessary for action to be responsible, but it strangles spontaneity: Agamemnon's image does not juxtapose two different kinds of action, rational and spontaneous, but suggests that an action which is somehow in itself spontaneous, organically developing, is meeting with obstruction when it actually emerges into the realm of human, practical activity. But seeing action in this way is part of the trouble: Agamemnon has unconsciously revealed the flaw in the very imagery he uses to talk about it. Agamemnon's conception of action is essentialist: he sees a project, a whole harmonious design, as somehow existing in itself, apart from the human beings involved in executing it; human action, according to this view, is merely an implementation of what is already wholly formed, somewhere below the surface of actuality. The project has to be 'embodied', as Ajax is seen as giving 'our project's life' a 'shape of sense', and breakdown between conception and embodiment is always possible. The Trojans see action as existential, and thus avoid the 'checks and disasters' of the Greeks, while running into others: for them, there is no gap between conception and execution, since the conception is only fully formed in the process of execution – Helen becomes meaningful in the process of fighting over her. Action for the Trojans is therefore spontaneous, conception and execution are united. But the elimination of the gap between conception and action can be the elimination of reason, of social responsibility: it is difficult to apply rational controls to pure spontaneity.

Spontaneity, too, is primarily personal, the expression of the individual's authentic impulses without obstruction. The Greeks think in terms of a project which involves them all, as a body: it is 'our works' which Agamemnon discusses. Action is social, and historical as well: the action of the present can be seen in logical continuity with actions of the past, and a comparison of past and present may clarify the situation: Agamemnon sees that the past projects of the Greeks, 'whereof we have record', have shown similar tendencies to the present. For the Trojans, action is individual and eternally present: the war is a personal exercise for them, a means to personal honour, and the past is 'strewn with husks', dead achievements. The Greeks, camped outside the city, see the war as a permanent condition: the Trojans sally out to the field and return to carry on their private lives in the city. Helen unites them, but it is their 'several honours', their 'joint and several dignities' which are engaged: they remain, essentially, individuals, seeing action as personal self-definition, brought temporarily together in the same quarrel. They are associated in the war, rather than bound, like the Greeks, into a single, interdependent community.

Both Troilus and Achilles disregard distinction and comparison, and in doing so reject reason. Troilus sees comparison as a base process:

> Fie, fie, my brother!
> Weigh you the worth and honour of a king,
> So great as our dread father's, in a scale
> Of common ounces?   (II, 2).

Achilles, Ajax and Thersites also reject rational processes, as Ulysses complains:

> They tax our policy and call it cowardice,
> Count wisdom as no member of the war,
> Forestall prescience, and esteem no act
> But that of hand. The still and mental parts
> That do contrive how many hands shall strike
> When fitness calls them on, and know, by measure
> Of their observant toil, the enemies' weight —
> Why, this hath not a finger's dignity . . .   (I, 3)

Troilus and Achilles both deny the rational, and thus the socially responsible, aspects of action; as a result, they gain in different ways a kind of authenticity, a truth-to-self and refusal to falsify, which in itself is valuable. The idea of intrinsic values, of rational weighing, can remain intact as long as it stays theoretical, inactive; as soon as it is put into operation it becomes a situation-ethics as relative and shifting as the fluid values of the Trojans. This is most evident in the actual political manœuvring of Ulysses and Nestor, in trying to induce Achilles to fight. The manœuvring is indeed governed by rational principle, by a careful weighing of the intrinsic merits of Achilles, Ajax, Hector, and their interrelations; but in practice it leads to a merely tactical attitude to life, stifling authenticity. Achilles, by comparison, has an attractive, if negative, integrity: in the light of Ulysses's cunning his disengagement can be seen, partially, as a refusal to surrender his integrity by entering the shifting flux of society. On these terms, integrity is only possible outside society: society manipulates a man into a social role, controls and defines him, and he can choose to reject this, to act by his private idea of himself. This choice is hardly conscious with Achilles, but in other plays it assumes great importance.

Troilus, too, can achieve authenticity only outside the network of weighed causes and consequences which is society. He creates, within society, an area of personal freedom where he can find himself fully: this area is his relationship with Cressida. The love-relationship with Cressida contains his authentic self, it is the way he defines himself; when Cressida is snatched away, he is alienated from himself. And it is society which snatches her away: his real self is destroyed by the pressures of a society which is seen as external, hostile to self-expression, which removes Cressida from him for rational, social reasons he sees as worthless.

The antagonism between 'reason' and 'intuition', between action based on rational weighing and action based on spontaneous impulse, is an antagonism between the 'social' and the 'authentic' self: between the way a man conceives of himself, and the way society tries to force him to see himself. Troilus is not merely an impetuous Romantic, although this is a possible level of reading: more deeply, he is committed, consciously, to expressing spontaneously his true self in action in a way which puts him outside the control of society:

> They that have the voice of lions and the act of hares, are they not monsters?   (III, 2)

Cressida's contemptuous question expresses the couple's shared belief: to make a dichotomy in oneself between impulse and execution is to make oneself deformed, monstrous. Living must be spontaneous, and therefore love becomes the archetypal way to live. But spontaneity is in fact constantly threatened, not only by the pressures of society, the demands of responsible and rational action, but by the nature of action itself. 'Activity' is fluid, spontaneous, self-expressive; 'act' is fixed, dead, confining. The ideal way to live would therefore consist in being constantly at the point of achievement without ever doing anything: at this moment, the self would be at its most authentic:

> Things won are done; joy's soul lies in the doing.   (I, 2)

As soon as desire is enacted, there is loss, deadness: the whole structure of the relationship of Troilus and Cressida – a passionate courtship, a brief consummation, a parting – makes this clear. 'Men prize the thing ungained more than it is' – there is a disparity, as there is with the projects of the Greeks, between the process and the end-product. To remain constantly at the point of achievement is impossible: some kind of commitment is sooner or later unavoidable. But for Troilus there is no one act sufficient to contain and express his whole self: he can define himself only by fluidity, as pure potential:

This is the monstruosity in love, lady, that the will is infinite, and the execution confin'd; that the desire is boundless, and the act a slave to limit.   (III, 2).

He knows himself only in terms of process: the result of tasting 'Love's thrice-repured nectar', of achieving sexual consummation, is death – 'swooning destruction'. This is why the sworn commitment of Troilus and Cressida to each other fails: it is an attempt to defeat flux made by two people who in fact see their reality as existential, as relative to the moment:

What's past and what's to come is strew'd with husks
And formless ruins of oblivion . . .   (IV, 5).

–Agamemnon's words to Hector apply equally to Troilus and Cressida: it is in the 'extant moment' that they find themselves.

But if spontaneity is opposed to the achieved self, it is opposed to society; for society is concerned with defining the individual in particular ways, assigning functions and roles. Troilus can only exist in an atomistic society like Troy: a man who sees himself in terms of process will escape from any fixed role, and his self-definition will be counter to society, not in terms of it. For Troilus, society is a hostile, repressive mechanism, threatening authentic fulfilment, crippling spontaneity: it is deadening, confining, as action itself is confining. And yet a man cannot totally escape from society, as an impulse cannot escape from hardening into act, sooner or later. Existence as pure potential, pure subjectivity, is ultimately impossible: the self becomes objectified in an action or a social role. Troilus's situation is therefore inherently tragic: he tries to act, in society, without ever seeing himself objectified in an action or a social role.

Social responsibility, then, seems to involve a distortion of spontaneity, a loss of authenticity: it demands reason and tactical skill, a willingness to accept others' definitions of oneself, an ability to see personal self-definition in terms of others and of a whole design. But the problem is that the man who rejects this, although irresponsible, will be, in a false society, the most genuine man: in refusing the definitions of society he will be asserting his real self, his authentic passion. To some extent, the irresponsibility follows inevitably from the whole situation: in a condition of general stagnancy, any assertion of personal creative life may be correspondingly violent and extreme, excessive in its overflow of spontaneity. Thersites makes the point implicitly in his first, biting words about Agamemnon:

> Agamemnon – how if he had boils full, all over, generally? . . . And those boils did run – say so. Did not the general run then? . . . Then there would come some matter from him; I see none now.   (II, 1)

The only creative movement of life possible from the stagnant and cerebral Agamemnon would, ironically, be an outpouring of pus, of evil matter. Even this, Thersites seems to suggest, might be preferable to total inactivity. Troilus's actions may be done without reflection, but he has in his spontaneity a wholeness which is lacking in the Greeks: he is capable of an integrity of self which contrasts favourably with the fragmented self of an Ajax, composed of other men's scraps.

But ultimately Shakespeare sides with reason, with social responsibility. Social responsibility may entail a damaging loss of authenticity, but it is the only way men can live together, for the moment. It is Diomed's opinion of Helen, not Troilus's, which he accepts:

> For every false drop in her bawdy veins
> A Grecian's life has sunk; for every scruple
> Of her contaminated carrion weight
> A Troyan hath been slain.   (IV, 1)

The weighing and balancing of drops and scruples is a vital process: this, finally, is the only way responsible human decisions can be reached. What is needed is a fusion of the passionate wholeness of Troilus and the rational responsibility of Ulysses; the search is for a way to make authentic energies socially responsible, to make social responsibility authentic and spontaneous. Ulysses's description of Troilus to Agamemnon is hopelessly wrong, but it points to the ideal requirement:

> . . . For what he has he gives, what thinks he shows,
> Yet gives he not till judgment guide his bounty . . .   (IV, 5)

It is 'bounty' which is admired, free and open self-giving which is authentic (he gives what he has and shows what he thinks, without distortion) and yet controlled by judgement.

Another way of seeing this necessary fusion is in Hector's terms, as an amalgam of intrinsic and conferred value. Value must draw its 'estimate and dignity' *both* from its intrinsic worth *and* from the judgement of the prizer: things must somehow be seen simultaneously as they are in themselves, and as they gain meaning in particular human contexts. Human creation and conferment of value is not rejected, but held in fusion with a recognition of inherent meanings. Reason examines these meanings and makes responsible decisions; spontaneity is a matter of human creation, human transfiguration of reality, as love transfigures the world.

This is easy to assert: but the play can find no way of making this fusion. Troilus, in trying to forge a permanent reality out of his love for Cressida, explores one possible fusion and finds it unsuccessful: he tries to make out of the humanly created value of love a reality as fixed and unchanging as a rational principle. He does this by making a vow, a commitment: but the vow has no rational foundation at all, it has to remain gratuitous. There is, indeed, a sense in which the gratuitousness is the foundation of the permanence: if there is no reason why a thing should not be willed to change, there is no reason why it should not be willed to remain the same. Love in this sense may be made more permanent than a rational action, since a rational action may alter according to changed circumstances, whereas love can be made, by a gratuitous act of will, impervious to what might reasonably alter it:

> . . . Love is not love
> Which alters when it alteration finds,
> Or bends with the remover to remove . . .   (Sonnet 116)

But because the commitment is gratuitous, not ratified by any rational principle, it can be abandoned: a total commitment is humanly made, and can be humanly broken.

The Greeks, too, try to fuse both kinds of value, by applying fixed, rational principles to existential situations. But all that happens is that the existential situations absorb the principles until they are fixed only in abstraction: the difference between Ulysses's theoretical statement of value and his actual practice makes this plain. The play ends with nothing decided: to be wise is to know things as they are through reason and thus act responsibly; to love is to create human meaning and act spontaneously. The two seem impossible to unite:

> . . . for to be wise and love
> Exceeds man's might; that dwells with gods above.   (III, 2)

CHAPTER TWO

Hamlet

THE plot of *Hamlet* turns on the fact that in Act I
Scene 5 Hamlet is given a task to fulfil by his father's
ghost – a task which he leaves undone until the very end
of the play. But this is only one of a number of assign-
ments which people lay on other people throughout the
play. Claudius appoints Cornelius and Voltemand as
ambassadors to the King of Norway, and Rosencrantz
and Guildenstern to discover the truth about Hamlet;
Polonius instructs Reynaldo to spy on Laertes, uses
Ophelia as bait to trap Hamlet, and is Claudius's self-
appointed agent; Hamlet orders Polonius to look after
the actors, and uses the actors as bait to catch Claudius;
Gertrude uses Rosencrantz, Guildenstern and Polonius
to bear messages to Hamlet, and Claudius uses Osric
for the same purpose; Claudius uses Laertes to kill
Hamlet, and Hamlet uses the English authorities to
get rid of Rosencrantz and Guildenstern; Horatio is
told by the dying Hamlet to give the succession of
Denmark to Fortinbras, and the play ends with Fortinbras's order for ceremonial shots to be fired. Messages
and reports are constantly being given by or about
one person to another via a third: Hamlet's friends tell
him about the Ghost; Ophelia tells Polonius about
Hamlet, and Polonius tells the King; Hamlet describes
his sea-voyage to Horatio; the Queen describes
Ophelia's death to Laertes. The process almost parodies

itself in Act IV Scene 6, where a message passes from
Hamlet to sailors to an attendant to Horatio to Claudius,
and Claudius's command before the duel images the
movement:

> . . . Give me the cups;
> And let the kettle to the trumpet speak,
> The trumpet to the cannoneer without,
> The cannons to the heavens, the heaven to earth,
> 'Now the King drinks to Hamlet'.   (V, 2)

Agency, then, is a central theme in *Hamlet*: society
is presented, and is present to each character, as a
continuous network of causes, agents, and effects, a
network of men reciprocally using and exploiting one
another. The reciprocity is important: men both use
others and are used, and as a result they have two senses
of themselves, as source and as agent (or object). Polonius is a professional go-between, almost at times a
pandar, but we see him also as a father, severe to
Ophelia, paternalistic to Laertes. Ophelia is used as a
pawn by Claudius and her father, but when she confronts Hamlet she forgets her role of agent and becomes
herself. Laertes is a source when advising Ophelia but
exploited as an agent by Claudius; Horatio executes
Hamlet's wishes but remains solid in his integrity, his
self-possession. Marcellus and Bernardo reduce themselves to dutiful agents in reporting the news of the
Ghost to Hamlet, but we have seen them already, in
the first scene of the play, as full, independent human
beings; even the players, who hardly move or speak
outside their role as actors, gain some independent
humanity from Hamlet's personal dealing with them.
Rosencrantz, Guildenstern and Osric, on the other

hand, have no existence at all outside their role as
agents. They are defined totally by the way society
uses them, and they accept and enact this definition,
seeing themselves as society sees them. This is especially evident in the case of Rosencrantz and Guildenstern, who consciously consign whatever integrity they
might have into Claudius's possession, as a free act:

> But we both obey,
> And here give up ourselves, in the full bent,
> To lay our service freely at your feet,
> To be commanded.   (II, 2)

Both men voluntarily surrender themselves to be controlled, and by actively consenting to being Claudius's
puppets they authenticate their appointed roles, make
them personally real; from this point on we see them
only in this function. Osric does not even personally
authenticate his role as agent: he is incapable even of
this degree of individual choice. He is whatever men
care to make him, an obedient reflection of other
men's views:

OSRIC I thank your lordship; it is very hot.

HAMLET No, believe me, 'tis very cold; the wind is northerly.

OSRIC It is indifferent cold, my lord, indeed.

HAMLET But yet methinks it is very sultry and hot for my
complexion.

OSRIC Exceedingly, my lord . . .   (V, 2)

Osric serves to hold the mirror up to nature, but the
image is not intended to shape the reality it reflects,
as Hamlet says an actor should do, as the mirror of
his own scorn shows Gertrude her vices. The agent

in *Hamlet* is not like the mediator in *Troilus and Cressida*: in *Troilus*, the mediator helps to create a new reality, actively shaping experience; in *Hamlet* the agent's task is to transmit what is entrusted to him intact to the receiver, cancelling his own identity in the process. This is what the clown in the graveyard scene refuses to do when questioned by Hamlet; he refuses to pass on information intact, colouring it constantly with his own personality:

HAMLET How came he mad?

CLOWN Very strangely, they say.

HAMLET How strangely?

CLOWN Faith, e'en with losing his wits.

HAMLET Upon what ground?

CLOWN Why, here in Denmark. I have been sexton here, man and boy, thirty years.   (V, 1)

The clown is all the time more concerned with exercising his wit than with giving Hamlet a straight answer; he can't keep himself out of the conversation, and turns the dialogue as soon as he can to himself. The scene immediately precedes Hamlet's encounter with Osric, and is meant to contrast with it: the clown asserts himself as an autonomous human being, causing Hamlet some dry amusement at his refusal to be servile; Osric has no humanity apart from his servility.

Throughout the play, the self as source and the self as agent (what A. P. Rossiter calls 'mind-sense' and 'self-sense')* are at odds: some men, like Claudius, appear almost totally autonomous, fulfilling themselves

* *'Angel with Horns'*, Longmans, Chapter 9.

by using others as agents, manipulating them into action; other men, like Osric, are objects, tools to be used. But generally the tension between self as subject and self as object is an interior one, between how a man sees himself, and his conception of how others see him or how he is actually used by others. Laertes has to be reduced carefully by Claudius from passionate self-affirmation to a pliable object capable of being turned against Hamlet; Ophelia lives at the point of tension between seeing herself as the obedient daughter of Polonius, subject to his will, and asserting her authentic self in her love for Hamlet: with her, the tension is finally destructive. Polonius consciously turns himself into an object, by becoming a self-appointed spy: he uses himself. Polonius's family provides a minor, reflecting image of the larger social network which includes it: Polonius is a source for Ophelia and Laertes, giving them both advice; Laertes is a source for Ophelia, advising her against receiving Hamlet's advances, but is suddenly objectified himself as Ophelia becomes herself a source, warning Laertes to obey his own advice.

The opposition is brought out in a peculiar way by a continual verbal play between 'eyes' or 'voice', and 'ears'. In the first scene, Marcellus wishes that Horatio will 'approve (their) eyes', confirm his experience, by seeing the Ghost which so far only he and Bernardo have seen: they tell him to sit down so that they may once more assail his ears. When Horatio finally sees the Ghost, he stresses the significance of his actual, personal seeing, as grounds for belief:

> Before my God, I might not this believe
> Without the sensible and true avouch
> Of mine own eyes. (I, 1)

and this contrasts with his mere half-belief in what he *hears*, when the story of the cock which sings all night at Christmas is told him:

So have I heard, and do in part believe it.

'Eyes' or 'voice', and 'ears', are used throughout the play as the symbols, respectively, for the self as subject and the self as object. It is what men see with their own eyes that is most genuinely personal: to look or speak is to act as subject. To hear is to become, even if only temporarily, an object, the passive recipient of another's subjective experience, and being reduced to this status of object can be dangerous: Laertes warns Ophelia not to receive Hamlet's overtures with 'too credent ear', and Ophelia in return reminds him to follow his own advice – to keep an adjustment between his subjective self and his public actions. Polonius's advice a few minutes later is the opposite: he warns Laertes to 'Give every man thine ear, but few thy voice', to make a conscious dislocation between his authentic, subjective self and the self which is present to others in the world.

The fact of the Ghost *speaking* to Hamlet also assumes importance, and the word is given emphasis; it is dumb to Marcellus and Bernardo, present to them only as an object; but it engages in dialogue with Hamlet, disclosing itself as a subject with a will. It makes him an object, calling on him to hear, and then lays a duty on him, making him an agent. The danger involved in being made into an object is revealed in the Ghost's account of his murder: the poison which killed him was poured in at the ear. A similar play between subject and object occurs in Act I Scene 2, where Gertrude appears to Hamlet to 'let (his) eye look like a friend on

Denmark', and a few minutes later Claudius echoes
her remark:

> . . . For your intent
> In going back to school in Wittenberg,
> It is most retrograde to our desire;
> And we beseech you bend you to remain
> Here, in the cheer and comfort of our eye. . .

Denmark is to be in Hamlet's eye, which means he is
to possess and control it as something which can be used
or enjoyed. But Hamlet, in turn, is to be in Claudius's
eye: controlled, defined by Claudius, assigned his
proper place at court, reduced perhaps to an object.
Men can put themselves at the mercy of others, sur-
rendering themselves up as Rosencrantz and Guildenstern do, in a kind of suicide, and later in the same scene
Hamlet warns Horatio against doing this, when Horatio
accuses himself of a truant disposition:

> I would not hear your enemy say so;
> Nor shall you do my ear that violence,
> To make it truster of your own report
> Against yourself.

A man's act can be taken from him and used against
him: by saying too much, by unpacking his heart
publicly, a man can hand himself into the control of a
listener, who then becomes a subject, manipulating
him as an object; Hamlet has just warned himself
before Horatio's entrance to hold his tongue. Words
can't be reclaimed: like all actions, they detach themselves from the performer, who can then disown responsibility for them but also lose control over their
consequences:

KING I have nothing with this answer, Hamlet; these words are not mine.

HAMLET No, nor mine now.   (III, 2)

Ophelia is warned by her father not to speak to Hamlet: a denial of speech, in this society, is a denial of self-giving, presenting oneself to the other merely as an object. Love, in these terms, is an engagement of two selves which does not demand the reduction of either to the status of objects,* and it is this which breaks down when Ophelia closes herself off from Hamlet, makes herself opaque to him. Ophelia tells Polonius of Hamlet's behaviour, and this information, 'given to (his) ear', he gives in turn to the ear of Claudius. Claudius hides himself to spy on Hamlet's encounter with Ophelia: he and Polonius

> Will so bestow ourselves that, *seeing unseen*,
> We may of their encounter frankly judge. . .   (III, 1)

'Seeing unseen' is the ideal situation for a man: he can be purely himself without being objectified by the look of another, as Hamlet feels himself seen and exploited when he becomes aware of Polonius in hiding. Claudius, generally in total control of others, a source and not an agent, rarely puts himself in a position where he can be reduced to an object; he is objectified in this way only twice in the play, once when he betrays himself during

---

* Real love, in the play, involves that knowledge of the centre of another which in this society is generally resisted because it is seen as an attempt to possess and objectify: Hamlet wears Horatio 'in his heart's core', Gertrude is 'conjunctive' to Claudius's 'heart and soul'. In contrast, Polonius's resolve to discover the truth about Hamlet 'though it were hid, indeed, within the centre' is an attempt to control him.

the play-scene under the scrutiny of Hamlet and Horatio ('Even with the very comment of thy soul,/Observe
my uncle'), and finally when he is stabbed by Hamlet
at the end of the play.

The conflict of self as subject and self as object
comes out strongly in Hamlet's confrontation of his
mother in Act III Scene 4. They begin as two subjects, each powerfully self-asserting and confident. The
quick, thrusting give-and-take of their opening duel
confirms this:

QUEEN Hamlet, thou hast thy father much offended.

HAMLET Mother, you have my father much offended.

QUEEN Come, come, you answer with an idle tongue.

HAMLET Go, go, you question with a wicked tongue.

The Conflict is equally balanced, the two selves directly
clashing: the reference in both cases is to 'tongues',
to the self as subject and source. Gertrude then tries to
gain control by a threat – 'Nay then, I'll set those to you
that can speak' – intended to reduce Hamlet to an
object, chastised by the voices of others. Hamlet sweeps
this aside with a direct command:

Come, come, and sit you down; you shall not budge.
You go not till I set you up a glass
Where you may see the inmost part of you.

He forces her, in physical posture, into a passive position, and rather than objectify her himself will be the
glass in which she will see herself as she is. Gertrude's
control breaks: she is reduced to fright and calls for
Polonius. But now Hamlet is completely in control, as

his cool response to Polonius's death indicates*: he shows his mother the portraits of her two husbands, noting the 'eye like Mars' of his father and describing Claudius as 'a mildew'd ear'. He cannot believe that Gertrude could have eyes and choose Claudius:

> Eyes without feeling, feeling without sight,
> Ears without hands or eyes, smelling sans all,
> Or but a sickly part of one true sense
> Could not so mope.

Even someone without a subjective, choosing self could hardly have been so blind. Gertrude is finally reduced to repentance:

> O Hamlet, speak no more!
> Thou turn'st my eyes into my very soul;
> And there I see such black and grained spots
> As will not leave their tinct.

Hamlet's words enter her ears like daggers, forcing her to objectify her sins. But the situation changes when the Ghost appears: now it is Hamlet who is objectified, both by the Ghost and by Gertrude. The Ghost objectifies both Hamlet and Gertrude, noting Gertrude's amazement and rebuking Hamlet for his delay; he tells Hamlet to reassure his mother, using him as an agent. Hamlet turns back to Gertrude, concerned for her, to find that she is concerned for him, objectifying him as mad. Each thinks the other is seeing wrongly: Gertrude thinks Hamlet is having hallucinations,

---

* Hamlet's reaction to Polonius's body, like his reaction to Yorick's skull, is to wonder at the distinction between the living, subjective self, and the dumb, objective corpse:

> . . . Indeed, this counsellor
> Is now most still, most secret, and most grave,
> Who was in life a foolish prating knave.

Hamlet can't understand why she can't see what to him is evidently there. The two selves clash again as subjects, asserting their own versions of seeing against each other. Finally Hamlet regains control: Gertrude submits to his advice and asks what she should do. But Hamlet's aim is a reconciliation, not merely a chance to reduce her to submission:

> Forgive me this my virtue;
> For in the fatness of these pursy times
> Virtue itself of vice must pardon beg,
> Yea, curb and woo for leave to do him good.

Hamlet wants to give Gertrude moral advice without reducing her to an object within his control: he wants, simultaneously, to have a real relationship with her. The only way he can achieve these conflicting ends, to see her both as subject and object, is to give her advice while asking her pardon for it: in this way he makes himself the object of her pardon as he makes her the object of his moralising.

Hamlet ends by laying on the Queen an injunction not to reveal to Claudius what he has said, and she assures him that she will be silent:

> Be thou assur'd, if words be made of breath
> And breath of life, I have no life to breathe
> What thou hast said to me.

Speech is deeply connected with personal life, with self-giving; Gertrude is not merely saying that she will repress what Hamlet has told her, but that her silence will be part of her deepest life, part of her truth-to-self: she makes Hamlet's restriction part of her authentic life as, in a different way, Rosencrantz and Guildenstern personally authenticate Claudius's commands.

Hamlet's last words to her are a reminder that he has to leave for England: it is he, now, who is to be used by others. But he intends to manipulate those who will try to control him:

> . . . Let it work;
> For 'tis the sport to have the engineer
> Hoist with his own petar; and't shall go hard
> But I will delve one yard below their mines
> And blow them at the moon.

Those who expect to use him as an object will find him an active subject, objectifying his manipulators:

> . . . O 'tis most sweet
> When in one line two crafts directly meet.

He expects a head-on collision of two subjective wills, each out to control the other, which was how his interview with his mother began.

More instances of the opposition of subject and object occur in the court's consternation at the death of Polonius. The corpse, Hamlet says, is at supper, 'not where he eats, but where he is eaten'. Eating provides a good image of the opposition: it has been used already in Hamlet's reference to Gertrude's lust as an increase of appetite growing from what it feeds on (I, 2). To feed is to use another creature as object to strengthen oneself as subject, and the process can be circular: 'we fat all creatures else to fat us, and we fat ourselves for maggots . . . a man may fish with the worm that hath eat of a king, and eat of the fish that hath fed of that worm.' All creatures simultaneously eat and are eaten, in endless reciprocity.

Laertes returns to Denmark, his ear 'infected' by 'buzzers'; he bursts in with an unruly crowd at his heels, over whom his control is shaky:

LAERTES Where is this king?—Sirs, stand you all without.

ALL No, let's come in.

LAERTES I pray you give me leave.

ALL We will, we will.   (IV, 5)

This is not just to show the crowd's fickleness: it reveals
again the tension of subject and object. Laertes can
gain a personal wish which is denied to him when he
appeals as subject to the crowd, by making himself
instead the object of their permission. Claudius,
similarly, lets Laertes rage on, and then begins to
direct the rage to his own ends, slowly, until Laertes is
ready to be commanded:

> My lord, I will be rul'd
> The rather, if you could devise it so
> That I might be the organ.   (IV, 7)

Laertes positively demands to become the King's agent,
his tool, because he sees this as a role within which he
can enact his own subjective resolution to kill Hamlet.
But from Claudius's viewpoint, Laertes as subject and
and as object are quite different: as Claudius's tool he
will be killing Hamlet for reasons entirely distinct from
his personal grievances.

When Laertes and Hamlet finally meet for the duel,
Hamlet tries to diminish the hostility by offering to
reduce himself to an object:

> I'll be your foil, Laertes; in mine ignorance
> Your skill shall, like a star i' th' darkest night,
> Stick fiery off indeed.   (V, 2)

In duelling, two selves come physically into conflict,
and the aim, for Laertes anyway, is to reduce Hamlet
to the purest objectivity possible to man, a corpse. The

reciprocity of the conflict is imaged in the changing of rapiers: Laertes stabs Hamlet with the poisoned blade, and is then stabbed with the same weapon. But Hamlet, even when dying, is a source rather than an agent: he kills Claudius, instructs Horatio to stay alive to tell his story, and gives his 'dying voice' to Fortinbras — he reaches out beyond his death as an active voice, transmitted in both Horatio and Fortinbras. The ambassadors from England comes too late with the news of the deaths of Rosencrantz and Guildenstern: the man who arranged their deaths has himself been killed, and 'the ears are senseless' to receive the information.

*   *   *

We can see the society of *Hamlet* as a continuous network of reciprocal human definitions, as we saw the society of *Troilus and Cressida*. As with *Troilus*, this inter-definition is felt both as limiting and circular: men's realities are reflected to them by the particular nexus of their society, and this can differ radically from the way they see themselves, from their authentic selves. In this condition, a man can either consent to finding his real self only in the margin of society, in non-official activities and relationships; he can sell himself over, alternatively, to the public definition, become as he is valued; or he can continue to assert his authentic life and risk destruction. In *Hamlet* we find all three experiments tried, and they are all inadequate.

The *Hamlet* society resembles the Greek camp in its enclosedness, its sense of the public eye, but it is a much more claustrophobic society, one riddled with spying and secrecy, with attempts to hunt down and possess the truth of others. In this context, self-repres-

sion is vital, just for survival: the fear and hesitancy of
the first scenes, the sense of concealed rottenness and
the doubt about the Ghost's identity, is part of the whole
atmosphere of a society where men are forced to close
themselves off from each other, falsifying their identities. To expose oneself is to risk manipulation, as
Polonius warns Ophelia: she must learn that being in
society, part of the complex network of cause and effect,
involves self-concealment. As a result, the tension between authentic desire and public role can become crippling: it can only be eased by inauthentic choosing, by
consenting to be an object, like Rosencrantz and Guildenstern. By actively choosing this self, they can mould
themselves to the required role, really become what
they are expected to be. Polonius, too, actively accepts
and authenticates his role as Claudius's tool, although
he allows himself some autonomy in the margin, in
the privacy of his family.

These are the terms, then, in which survival in Denmark is possible, and they are the terms available to
Hamlet as well as to everyone else. Hamlet has a particular function in society – that of prince – and the
specific function, given to him by his father, of killing
Claudius. But Hamlet, like Troilus, conceives of himself as pure fluidity: like Achilles, his whole character
is geared to resisting any externally imposed definition.
The first time we see him he is concerned to point out
that he is something more than he appears, that there
is a discontinuity between his real self, and the objective
self present to the world: forms, moods and shapes
cannot denote him truly, for

> . . . I have that within which passes show—
> These but the trappings and the suits of woe. (I, 2)

This, in the whole context of the play, is more than a
rejection of the specifically distorting appearances of
mourning: it is also a rejection of any attempt to be fully
identified. It is not just that black garments can falsify
the self: any posture at all, any particular commitment,
is in itself falsifying because it seems to deny the possibility of other postures. Like Troilus, Hamlet's self
can be defined only in terms of process: the disowning
of 'appearances' is, more deeply, the disowning of any
particular action as an adequate image of self. This is
the real motivation behind the twisting, evasive conversation, the cryptic comments and disowning of im-
puted attitudes. Hamlet deliberately confuses others
about his real self, creating several different versions
which refuse to mesh into a single image.

Hamlet, like Claudius, is a source rather than an
agent, and it is this which Claudius recognises as
dangerous: he is a difficult man to manipulate. The
court find Hamlet impenetrable: they are disturbed
both by his silence, his cryptic, uncommunicative presence at their proceedings, and by the evasive, fast-
talking self he reveals when he breaks out of this shell.
Hamlet uses both methods to keep the court at bay,
to resist any imposed definition from outside: he refuses
objectification both by shifting his ground so quickly
that it is impossible to pin him down (as in his banter
with Polonius, and his interchange with Ophelia in the
play-scene), and by keeping silent, by withholding his
real self and thus staying untrapped:

You would play upon me; you would seem to know my stops;
you would pluck out the heart of my mystery. . . . 'Sblood, do
you think I am easier to be play'd on than a pipe? Call me what

instrument you will, though you can fret me, yet you cannot play upon me.   (III, 2)

Hamlet's fine, fluid mind is amusedly indignant that Rosencrantz and Guildenstern should have so low an opinion of him as to think that he could actually be fully known to them as a man: he breaks free of any definition the court can provide, as he breaks out of the restraining arms of his friends to follow the Ghost. Those who can be fully known, whose real selves are fully embodied in their objective functions and roles, are inauthentic men like Osric, assembled by society; on these terms, the real man is the one who can keep something of himself in reserve, who can retain some integrity. This means a willingness to be inactive, to avoid full involvement with the world. To be fully involved is to be fully known, completely available to others and therefore vulnerable, exposed to exploitation. A real man, for Hamlet, is one who can only be described in terms of himself:

> . . . I take him to be a soul of great article, and his infusion of such dearth and rareness as, to make true diction of him, his semblable is his mirror, and who else would trace him, his umbrage, nothing more.   (V, 2)

Horatio's reply in Act I Scene 1 to Marcellus's question 'Is it not like the King?', referring to the Ghost, is 'As thou art to thyself': the ultimate criterion of similarity is a man's own absolute likeness to himself. Comparison with others, for Hamlet, is part of that whole process of public judgements which forms the basis of the Greek sense of identity in *Troilus*, and which Cressida and Pandarus come to reject for an essentialist, individualist view of men as beings-in-themselves, unique.

Hamlet's deliberately meaningless communication to his eager friends after the Ghost has left him —

> There's never a villain dwelling in all Denmark
> But he's an arrant knave.   (I, 5)

— is an echo of this feeling that men can be defined only in relation to themselves. But this process, like the inter-definition of a whole society, is closed and circular: as in *Troilus*, both ways of living are inadequate. Polonius comes close to the same sense of things-in-themselves when he announces to the King and Queen that true madness is to be nothing else but mad: to describe it further would be as pointless as trying to explain why day is day and night night. Things are as they are, independent of human valuations: Hamlet's melancholy leads him to see the sky as a pestilent congregation of vapours and man as a quintessence of dust, but he recognises this for what it is, a personal feeling, a personal interpretation:

> I am but mad north-north-west; when the wind is southerly
> I know a hawk from a handsaw.   (II, 2)

The self can be defined only with reference to itself, because it is always deeper and more complex than any of its manifestations in action in the public world. For this reason, the common process of judgement and evaluation of the individual which was the mainspring of the Greek view of society in *Troilus* is rejected: the authentic individual is always ultimately behind and beyond his actions as they are present to others, and their judgement can therefore only ever be partial. Hamlet's contempt for the common judgement comes out in his contempt for the 'general', the theatre audiences whose judgement must always be ignored in favour of the opinions of a few, select men. We see, in this kind of attitude, how close his rejection of social definition is to a generally aristocratic stance, a feeling that full involvement in a social role is crudely limiting, that the true man will always keep some distance between himself and his actions. A full definition of an authentic man is as impossible as a definition of a ghost; indeed the wonder and questioning of Marcellus and Bernardo when confronted with the Ghost reflects the attitude of the court to Hamlet himself. The Ghost is present to Marcellus and Bernardo only as an object, dumb and mysterious; but it has, also, all the fluid evasiveness of pure subjectivity, in a quite physical sense: it appears suddenly, without warning, and seems to dissolve into the air:

> We do it wrong, being so majestical,
> To offer it the show of violence;
> For it is, as the air, invulnerable,
> And our vain blows malicious mockery.   (I, 2)

Marcellus's words, stretched a little, could almost be taken as applying to Hamlet: this is essentially the way the court sees Hamlet, as a figure invulnerable in his elusiveness, and it is Horatio's ability to take the buffets and rewards of Fortune with equal thanks that Hamlet most admires in him. Hamlet 'eats the air', as he remarks to Claudius (III, 2), a comment which echoes Marcellus's remark about the Ghost. When Hamlet encounters the Ghost, he compares it to himself:

> I do not set my life at a pin's fee;
> And for my soul, what can it do to that,
> Being a thing immortal as itself?   (I, 4)

Hamlet sets his physical existence in society at nothing; but his real self, his soul, is as immortal as the Ghost itself.

The play begins by creating a sense of fluidity, hesitation, doubt: the quick, confused questioning of the sentries, the anxious mutual establishment of identity, leads on to the doubt about the Ghost and the uncommitted scepticism of Horatio. Doubt is expressed in terms of a number of open possibilities:

> If thou hast any sound or use of voice,
> Speak to me.
> If there be any good thing to be done,
> That may to thee do ease and grace to me,
> Speak to me.
> If thou art privy to thy country's fate,
> Which happily foreknowing may avoid,
> O speak! ...   (I, 1)

and Hamlet's later questioning of the Ghost echoes this:

> Be thou a spirit of health or goblin damn'd,
> Bring with thee airs from heaven or blasts from hell,
> Be thy intents wicked or charitable,
> Thou com'st in such a questionable shape
> That I will speak to thee.*   (I, 4)

It is speaking, mutual engagement in dialogue, which establishes meaning and identity: this is why both Horatio and Hamlet emphasise the importance of speaking so much. Until speech is established and the

---

* The same sense of a number of possibilities, a fluidity, is there in Polonius's announcement of the actors' programme: 'tragedy, comedy, history, pastoral, pastoral-comical, historical-pastoral . . . (II, 2). The actors, like Hamlet, have identities which are completely flexible, capable of any posture.

self disclosed, the other exists only in terms of a number of possibilities, or as an object, impenetrable to enquiry. Hamlet's encounter with Gertrude in Act III Scene 4 is seen by him as this kind of direct and ultimate grappling with another, a final establishment of the truth: it is deliberately a high-point, a set piece, a confrontation in which Hamlet is determined to break through to the truth of his mother, to wring her heart 'if it be made of penetrable stuff'.

The Ghost's evasiveness, then, is of two kinds, like Hamlet's: it has a fluidity which evades localisation (' 'Tis here! . . . 'Tis here! . . . 'Tis gone!'), a ubiquitousness (it is '*Hic et ubique*', in Hamlet's words, everywhere at once, following Hamlet's shifts of ground); it is also, at first, a dumb object, resisting enquiry. These two conditions are imaged respectively in its two different states of being: during the night it wanders, during the day it is confined in the prison-house of purgatory. Its self-disclosure to Hamlet has to be made quickly, before it is forced to return to confinement; when it confronts Marcellus, Bernardo and Horatio, it is caught at the point of tension between self-disclosure in speech and the pressures which draw it back into prison and silence. The tension is essentially the one we have seen in other characters, between the self as subject and as object, between free self-giving and self-concealment. The Ghost as subject is 'extravagant and erring', but in this condition it can speak and be known for what it is; imprisoned in purgatory it is dumb. It fades on the point of action, of speech: it fails, at first, to realise itself in free disclosure, and even when it talks to Hamlet it is continually aware of the pressures of purgatory at work, drawing it back.

The Ghost's appearance reduces Marcellus and Barnardo to a fluidity like its own, making them incapable of action:

> . . . thrice he walk'd
> By their oppress'd and fear-surprised eyes,
> Within his truncheon's length; whilst they, distill'd
> Almost to jelly with the act of fear,
> Stand dumb and speak not to him.   (I, 2)

The jelly to which Marcellus and Bernardo are reduced is like the dew into which Hamlet wishes his too-solid flesh would dissolve: it is a state of pure subjectivity which is incapable of objectifying itself in action. This is the condition in which Hamlet lives throughout the play, resisting the objectification of action and a fixed social role. He is a source, not an agent or an object: when Polonius brings him the news of the actors' arrival his reply is 'Buzz, buzz' – stale news. He is not the kind of man to be given news by Polonius: he knows it already. Polonius is not even allowed the minute degree of power over Hamlet which telling him something he did not know before would involve. In their encounter in Act II Scene 2, Hamlet refuses to be Polonius's agent even in the most basic sense of giving straight answers to questions seeking information: like the clown, he twists the questions and throws back ambiguous answers, reducing the questioner to confusion, exploiting him. Laertes's view of Hamlet, expounded to Ophelia, is thus powerfully ironic:

> . . . Perhaps he loves you now,
> And now no soil nor cautel doth besmirch
> The virtue of his will; but you must fear,
> His greatness weigh'd, his will is not his own;

For he himself is subject to his birth:
He may not, as unvalued persons do,
Carve for himself; for on his choice depends
The sanity and health of this whole state;
And therefore must his choice be circumscrib'd
Unto the voice and yielding of that body
Whereof he is the head.   (I, 3)

To Laertes, Hamlet must be taken as a man only within the public role which officially identifies him: he must confine his authentic life within this public definition, making himself what society makes him. His choices and actions must be socially responsible, answerable to the whole society whose values he should focus and shape. But Hamlet does, in fact, carve for himself all the time: by evading the formal definitions society lays on him, by cutting through expected behaviour and approaching Ophelia with a directly personal appeal after the shock of the Ghost's announcement, he is acting counter to the patterns prescribed for him: his 'authentic' and 'social' selves, his own sense of himself and the way others see him, are at odds.

Society denies Hamlet authenticity: it asks him to surrender up his own desires, his love for Ophelia and his reluctance to be limited by a fixed role, and take on an official function. Life on these terms, on the terms of Osric and Rosencrantz and Guildenstern, is clearly unacceptable for Hamlet: he is intent on not being a puppet. But Hamlet's insistence on not being a puppet leads, finally, to a delight in resisting any kind of definition: it becomes, in fact, socially irresponsible, a merely negative response. This is the really tragic tension in the play, the central dilemma. The significant actions which are available to Hamlet as formal modes of self-definition, the actions of killing Claudius and behaving as prince, are not the actions in which he can find himself authentically; therefore he is unable to act. But the real tragedy of a man who is unable to find self-definition within formal social patterns, who can preserve his sense of identity only in opposition to these patterns, is that this identity then becomes unreal, negative. A self which can know itself only in constant opposition to its context finally destroys itself. This is the savage irony of the authentic man in a false society, the irony, to some degree, of Achilles in *Troilus*; the man who can find himself only outside his society's terms will disintegrate because of his very lack of that offered social verification of his existence which he is rejecting as false. Society may indeed be seen as false, its offered definitions as distorting, but it is still the only available way for a man to confirm himself as real, to objectify and know himself in public action. A man who does not objectify himself in action becomes unreal, as Achilles, according to Ulysses, is unreal; he loses, too, that spontaneity and truth-to-self which is the very ground of his opposition to the society.

This is Hamlet's situation. Hamlet must refuse to act in the public ways open to him because they seem to him false definitions of himself; but his refusal to act means that he begins to lose hold on his identity, to lose spontaneous life. He turns from the public roles and actions to the personal relationship with Ophelia, looking there for a kind of definition, to find that this too has been absorbed into the public pattern: Ophelia has made an inauthentic choice, like Rosencrantz and Guildenstern, she has wavered between Polonius and Hamlet and chosen the former. Hamlet, now, cannot even find the authentic self-expression he is looking for in the margins of society: he is stirred into spontaneous life only momentarily, with Horatio or the actors. He can now preserve his integrity only by evading the offered definitions, and this involves a state of constant fluidity: to be himself he must keep himself free from the limiting demands of society, he must keep one jump ahead all the time. But the effort of doing this, para-doxically, is destructive of the very integrity he hopes to preserve; he, like the court, becomes involved in secretive and calculating politics, only in his case the politics, ironically, is a way of staying free from the machinations of the others. In a false society, there are a number of ways of preserving integrity, but they are all self-defeating. A man, to avoid the exploitation of others, may make himself opaque, refuse self-disclosure in action, as Hamlet does; but to refuse action is to stagnate, to lose spontaneity. He may, on the other hand, try to play the society's game of manipulation, and by playing it better than they do hoist them with their own petard; again, this involves a surrender of integrity, a sharing in the shifty tactics of others. Hamlet does this, and becomes like Claudius:

> HAMLET 'Tis dangerous when the baser nature comes
> Between the pass and fell incensed points
> Of mighty opposites.
>
> HORATIO Why, what a king is this!   (V, 2)

Hamlet is completely trapped: he can find authenticity neither within nor outside society, since both to step outside the official nexus of the court, and to commit himself to it, involves loss of integrity, disintegration.

Hamlet's society is characterised by Claudius's first

speech to the court in Act I Scene 2. It is, above all, a society which weighs and measures, balancing consequences according to a fixed and rational scale of values: Claudius has weighed delight and dole in equal scale, considered additional factors like the opinions of the court, and made a decision: his efficient mind, moving easily from topic to topic, is offended by the disproportion of Hamlet's obstinate persistence in grief. For Claudius, feeling and action must be adjusted, according to reason; Hamlet, like Troilus, emphasises the human response, the human energy:

POLONIUS My lord, I will use them according to their desert.

HAMLET God's bodykins, man, much better. Use every man after his desert, and who shall scape whipping? Use them after your own honour and dignity: the less they deserve, the more merit is in your bounty.   (II, 2).

Hamlet rejects the ethic of rational weighing, as Troilus does, in favour of a free, spontaneous self-giving which disturbs rational calculations. This is a viewpoint which the society cannot tolerate: it is bounty, free self-giving, which Laertes and Polonius criticise in Ophelia: she must be chary of herself, not prodigal, set her entreatments at a 'higher rate'. To act spontaneously, disproportionately, is to be vulnerable, to overstep the safe limits of social role and expose one's true self freely, without balanced calculation. This can be socially disruptive: for society to function, men must suit the action to the word and the word to the action, as Hamlet reminds the player; like clowns and ambassadors, men must not speak more than is set down for them. The contrast is between spontaneous self-expression and reflective restraint, between the pure, fluid freedom of the subjective self, and the defined, known limits of the self as object.

The society of *Hamlet* lacks spontaneous life: men have to stifle themselves in the interests of the State. But this, at least, means that action can be socially responsible, in a way that spontaneous action often is not. It is Guildenstern, the hollow man, who seals Hamlet's death-warrant with his reminder that kingship is a massy wheel, to whose spokes ten thousand lesser things are adjoined: the symbol of social responsibility is one of unity, coherence. Hamlet is described in terms of diffusion: his sighs seem to Ophelia to 'shatter all his bulk', the Ghost warns him that his 'knotted and combined locks' will part, 'and each particular hair stand on end', when he hears his story. The tragedy of the authentic man in a false society is that he is driven into a position where his authenticity becomes negative, a cynical withdrawal from all commitment, from responsibility. For Hamlet, as for Achilles, society becomes merely stuff for personal self-expression, old men to be parodied. Like Troilus, Hamlet is a man who sees himself in terms of process, and who therefore resists social function; subjectivity refuses to be objectified and becomes self-consuming. It is the deadlock of *Troilus* again, the incompatibility of authentic and responsible action, of action-for-self and action-for-others. To be true to oneself, to preserve integrity, may well involve falseness to others, in spite of what Polonius says.

CHAPTER THREE

Measure for Measure

Measure for Measure is about the opposition between law and passion, but nothing in the play can really be understood unless the full significance of 'law' is grasped. Law can be seen as an essential restraint on individual action, and thus as a negative force: it is seen like this frequently in the play, both by those who dispense justice and by those who are its victims. But law has a positive aspect as well, one which makes criticism of those who break the law deeper and more subtle.

In Act I Scene 2, Claudio is arrested for having illegal sexual relations with Julietta, who is now pregnant by him:

> Thus stands it with me: upon a true contract
> I got possession of Julietta's bed.
> You know the lady: she is fast my wife,
> Save that we do the denunciation lack
> Of outward order . . .

The contract by which Claudio gained possession of Julietta's bed may have been true, but it was a private one, made between themselves and without the sanction of society. The results of their private encounters have now broken out into the open, into public view:

> The stealth of our most mutual entertainment,
> With character too gross, is writ on Juliet.

Their act stands exposed to the judgement of society, and Claudio is condemned by law. But Claudio's way of viewing his own offence is inadequate: he submits to the law's censure but fails to see the real point of the law, its function in verifying private experience, giving social confirmation or censure to individual action. Instead, he sees society's action in condemning him primarily in terms of the personality of the new deputy, Angelo, who is using him as a test case. His inability to understand the real meaning of law is reflected in his angry comment to the Provost: 'Fellow, why dost thou show me thus to the world?' (I, 2); he misses the whole point of law and judgement, which is precisely that it must be public or nothing. As the play demonstrates, 'the denunciation of outward order' is not a marginal element in human action, as Claudio sees it, an additional seal to an already firm contract; until individual action is ratified by society, the private contract does not properly exist. Ulysses in *Troilus* would have seen this immediately: personal action, to be real, must be available for social verification. Marriage is a public commitment, a way of relating personal behaviour to a whole society; its physical results are part of that society, children. Claudio and Julietta have ignored this, treating sexuality as a private affair, and their own act has turned against them in Julietta's evident pregnancy. Claudio is condemned not merely for lechery, but for breaking social order by concealing personal action from society's evaluation, trying to live a private reality beyond the law and thus beyond others. Sexual activity, which is at once intimately personal and directly social, is an ideal image of this theme.

The starting-point of the play, then, as I have suggested, is Ulysses's speech to Achilles in *Troilus and Cressida:*

> . . . no man is the lord of anything . . .
> Till he communicate his parts to others;
> Nor doth he of himself know them for aught
> Till he behold them formed in th'applause
> Where th'are extended . . .   (III, 3).

Personal identity, personal action, live only in that formal network of communications which is society. This is the meaning of the Duke's remark to Angelo at the beginning of the play:

> . . . Thyself and thy belongings
> Are not thine own so proper as to waste
> Thyself upon thy virtues, they on thee.
> Heaven doth with us as we with torches do,
> Not light them for themselves; for if our virtues
> Did not go forth of us, 'twere all alike
> As if we had them not . . .   (I, 1)

A man who conceals his qualities wastes himself, in a self-consuming process; the alternatives are self-hoarding or self-spending, free self-giving in action. A man is given natural qualities which he must use and communicate in action, otherwise they hardly exist: he can only know himself in this process of communication. Men are stewards for Nature, responsible to her for their action: Nature hates waste, and demands back from men in precise measure the gifts she lends him:

> Spirits are not finely touch'd
> But to fine issues; nor Nature never lends
> The smallest scruple of her excellence
> But, like a thrifty goddess, she determines
> Herself the glory of a creditor,
> Both thanks and use.   (I, 1)

There is a poetic tension in this between precision and freedom, scruples and excellence: men must expend freely the qualities Nature gives them, but this bounteousness must take place within the context of a precise weighing, a balancing of credit and debit. Free self-giving must co-exist with a kind of responsibility, to Nature or heaven or society: it is this responsibility which Claudio and Julietta ignore.

The Duke's resignation of government to Angelo and Escalus at the beginning of the play is also done in terms of a fullness of self-expression within a specific responsibility. The Duke tells Escalus that he has no need to recount the properties of government, since Escalus already has full and sufficient knowledge of the science; but he adds a restriction:

> . . . The nature of our people,
> Our city's institutions, and the terms
> For common justice, y'are as pregnant in
> As art and practice hath enriched any
> That we remember. There is our commission,
> From which we would not have you warp.   (I, 1)

The final sentence jars slightly: Escalus is praised for his sufficiency, for a fullness described in terms of richness and pregnancy, but in spite of this he must keep to the Duke's design: his richness of knowledge must find expression only within these terms. The Duke then turns to Angelo and praises him for a quality of character which makes him fully available to the observer:

> There is a kind of character in thy life
> That to th'observer doth thy history
> Fully unfold.

Angelo is praised as a genuine man, one whose public actions and private self are in complete continuity. He is then given his commission by the Duke:

> In our remove be thou at full ourself;
> Mortality and mercy in Vienna
> Live in thy tongue and heart . . .

Angelo is asked to be fully the Duke, to take on his identity, and thus to take on full sovereignty. This involves at once a fullness and a restriction, a freedom of self-expression and a conformity to a specific pattern of behaviour. Angelo is to become the Duke, to make his own self into someone else's: his scope will be as the Duke's, which means he will have freedom to enforce the laws as seems good to his own soul. So there will be no tension between his own desires and the received commission: by making himself fully into the Duke, by personally authenticating the new role, he can find full freedom for his real self, making it correspond completely with the delegated function. He will *be* the function, as completely as the Duke is himself. To fall short of the function, to become corrupt, will thus be falling short of the Duke, and therefore of himself: it will be not merely a failure in responsibility but a loss of authenticity, since the two have become identified in him. He has been given the full freedom of sovereignty, of wisdom: to go beyond this freedom, then, can only be a negative act, a falling short: too much freedom is loss of freedom, as Claudio makes clear in his rueful comment to Lucio. Claudio has overreached himself, and been arrested as the result of too much liberty:

As surfeit is the father of much fast,
So every scope by the immoderate use
Turns to restraint. Our natures do pursue,
Like rats that ravin down their proper bane,
A thirsty evil; and when we drink we die.   (I, 2)

Angelo, then, is being asked to make personally his the pattern of behaviour which the Duke epitomises, so that his personal action, his real self, will exist only in these terms. And what the Duke epitomises is law, the pattern of social responsibility. The law is to be Angelo's authentic life, so that it will be natural and spontaneous for him to think and act within its terms: he will be a living fusion of social responsibility and authentic, spontaneous self-expression. In him they will be the same life: to be less than good will be to be less than himself.

This is not, of course, how Claudio or Lucio see the law. For Claudio, the law is an external, repressive force, designed to interfere with personal self-fulfilment in the interests of society: it is a regrettable necessity. Lucio doesn't even recognise the necessity: for him, law is merely external, a ludicrous piece of official mechanism which has no relation to the realities of life, the living experience of wit or sex or compassion. As a result, Lucio's view of life is completely private: he lives in the margin of society, contemptuous of the public world, outside the network of roles and relationships. His instinct is always to choose the close, private contact against the public, the institutional:

Marry, sir, I think, if you handled her privately, she would sooner confess; perchance, publicly, she'll be ashamed.   (V, 1)

Because of this his experience is fragmentary, like his speech: he responds to the moment, creating a reality as he goes along, forging an identity in his conversation and then denying it later, attributing his own words to others. Because he fails to see the significance of law, he cannot see the need for that settled network of relationships which law should order and create: he lacks that sense of 'a dependency of thing on thing', the sense of constant value and relation, which is the quality in Isabella's speech that persuades the Duke she is not a mad woman (V, 1). To deny law is to deny society, to reject public experience; but it is only within the controlling network of law and society that individual experience can have meaning. Law is the articulation of the relations between things: particularly of the relations between private and public experience, personal behaviour and society, self and others. Without law, personal experience can only remain fragmentary, socially irresponsible.

Law is a positive force, then, because ideally it is not just part of a society, but actually *constitutes* society: it is a body of communications between men which makes their personal experience present to each other for verification, and thus brings them into relationship with each other; being a member of a society is defined by keeping its laws.* In this way, law is very similar to language, and the play brings out, implicitly, the connection. Both law and language are communications which bring men into relationship and community by externalising their private experience, making it

---

* This is not, of course, true of the law in Vienna as the Duke has left it: the law, because it has not been used publicly, has become dead, as private experience without social verification is dead:

    . . . so our decrees,
    Dead to infliction, to themselves are dead . . . (I, 3)
The law can only become dynamic, alive to itself, by being communicated.

open to public judgement and response. This is why
there is so great an emphasis, throughout the play, on
the fact of speech. Lucio's lack of respect for law is
closely tied to his lack of respect for language: both
law and language make a man social, relate him dyna-
mically to a society. Lucio lies constantly, creating
images for their own sake, using language as a means of
private enjoyment:

> Some report a sea-maid spawn'd him; some, that he was begot
> between two stock-fishes. But it is certain that when he makes
> water his urine is congeal'd ice; that I know to be true. And he
> is a motion generative; that's infallible.   (III, 2)

Lucio's slanderous tongue runs on, spinning words
irresponsibly, shifting ground opportunistically, piling
up ideas as they occur to him and then offering them as
constant truth. It is his over-readiness to speak which
the Duke condemns in the final judgement scene*: his
familiar sin, as he says to Isabella, is to 'seem the lapwing, and to jest, tongue far from heart' (I, 4). The
connection between flightiness (the lapwing) and falsehood is important: language, like law, must be constant,
commonly shared and therefore not open to personal
distortion; it is constant because it is common, as laws
are common and cannot be bent at will by individuals
to suit a situation. Lucio is flighty in speech, and his
language defines and expresses his whole, opportunist
character, his tactical approach to life. His lack of

---

* By contrast, the Provost's generosity is reflected in his readiness to give
speech freely, and to give more than is precisely necessary:

> DUKE Provost, a word with you.
> PROVOST As many as you please.   (III, 1)

and he is willing to do more than the Duke requires, 'if more were needful'
(II, 3).

respect for language is a lack of respect for the public world: his public presence, in his speech, is at odds with his real intentions, he is an inauthentic man.

The parallel between a personal distortion of language and a distortion of law is brought out interestingly in Elbow's misuse of words in Act II Scene 1. Elbow continually gets words wrong, using 'detest' for 'attest', 'cardinally' for 'carnally', and this provides much of the scene's humour; but in the context of the whole play it has a more serious, thematic meaning. Elbow puts personal interpretations on words, using them according to a scheme of private meaning, and the result is parallel to what Angelo does with the law: those who bid the law, or language, 'make curtsey to their will' cause a breakdown in social communication, one which may be small and comical in the case of Elbow, but immensely serious in Angelo's case.

If words are used existentially, differently in different contexts, then no fixed and constant meaning is possible, and no consistent value or communication: inconstancy strikes at the root of society. When Isabella is arguing for Claudio's life, she argues on this kind of shifting, relative basis, in the face of Angelo's inhuman constancy: she uses a situation-ethics, an individualist kind of value, as Troilus did:

> We cannot weigh our brother with ourself.
> Great men may jest with saints: 'tis wit in them;
> But in the less foul profanation.   (II, 2)

Isabella's rejection of the possibility of weighing and comparing two people, like Cressida's, is a contracting-out of the whole process of public evaluation and the rational establishment of value, an obstinate stand on individuality, uniqueness. But then this becomes the basis of a total relativism: if things lack the intrinsic values which make comparison possible, they become wholly dependent, for meaning and value, on their contexts; the same jest may be wit in one man and profanation in another. Isabella goes on to emphasise her argument:

> That in the captain's but a choleric word
> Which in the soldier is flat blasphemy.

A word's meaning depends on who speaks it: there can be no constancy, the constancy which comes from comparing and relating different experiences. Isabella's final attack is precisely in Troilus's terms: she says she will bribe Angelo,

> Not with fond sicles of the tested gold,
> Or stones, whose rate are either rich or poor
> As fancy values them; but with true prayers . . .

The echo of Troilus's 'What's aught but as 'tis valued?' is significant: a sense of value as lying primarily in the human response is part of that whole relativism which destroys the continuity of formulated law and language. Angelo's attitude to Isabella's pleading is quite firm: he cannot make an individual exception, because this demolishes the whole meaning of law. Law cannot operate as a kind of situation-ethics, relative to individual and context, any more than language can be altered to suit the whims of individual men.

The breakdown which Lucio sees between law and experience is a breakdown, also, between experience and language. In a good society, there will be a fine adjustment between what is thought and what is said, between private experience and public action. Language is action, present objectively to others in the public world: it must therefore carry the authentic self of the speaker, if breakdown is to be avoided. The measure to which a man is present in his words is the measure to which his public and private selves will be in continuity: the Duke cannot see himself 'live' in Lucio's descriptions of him. The measure to which one's personal, spontaneous behaviour is lawful will be, similarly, a measure of continuity between the authentic self and the social self, the self which society desires a man to be. Those who experience a breakdown between language and meaning are living a breakdown between personal experience and public function: Angelo, when he falls from integrity, cannot put himself into his language any more, his tongue becomes detached from his heart.

The image of tongue and heart recurs constantly throughout the play. The Duke tells Angelo to let the government of Vienna live in his tongue and heart – in both his public and his private selves, so that these will be one. Lucio tells Isabella that the Duke's 'givings-out' about his intentions 'were of an infinite distance from his true-meant design' (I, 4); Isabella forbids Angelo's tongue to sound a thought against Claudio if he finds that his heart is guilty. When Angelo tries to play, his 'invention' anchors on Isabella, and heaven receives empty words: the evil conception is growing in his heart. In the final judgement scene, the Duke's rebuke of Isabella's vehement description of Angelo as 'this pernicious caitiff deputy' is answered when she assures him that 'the phrase is to the matter'. The adjustment must be between heart and tongue, private and public selves, description and experience: Isabella's words are in precise proportion to the subject-matter, whereas Lucio's are dangerously excessive.

The idea of proportion, of fitting the word to the action and the action to the word, is a central one in the play, as the title makes clear. The whole man, the man of integrity, will be one whose public presence, in language and action, will be a real, authentic expression of himself, without jar or dislocation; this is the meaning of spontaneity, the ability of a man to give himself fluently to the world, without tension or falsification. But action must be socially responsible as well as spontaneous: wholeness is to be authentically lawful, spontaneously responsible, as Angelo is meant to be. The idea of a proportion between the inward and the public self, experience and action, is close, also, to the idea of proportion between crime and punishment: a man must 'answer' for his deed, otherwise the whole balance of society is upset. Gratuitous, individual forgiveness upsets the balance: there must be weighing and reckoning, measure for measure. Angelo is 'precise', and the word occurs several times in the play: he believes that there must be proportion, not only between what a man is and what he does, but between what he does and society's response to this.

Angelo, to begin with, is totally authentic: there is no dislocation at all between himself and his actions, between what he is and what he does.* He represents the living fusion of responsibility and authenticity which

* Later, of course, we learn that he has in fact all along been in the same position as Claudio and Julietta: he has made a private contract (with Mariana) which he has not allowed to be publicly ratified. He is thus seriously inauthentic in this respect, but this fact does not interfere with our response to him at the beginning of the play.

we described earlier: he lives personally in terms of the law, of socially responsible behaviour. But total integrity of this kind can be destructive and inhuman, based on a rejection of human experience. Angelo's impatient reply to Isabella's insistent questioning exposes the ruthlessness of his spontaneity:

ANGELO I will not do't.

ISABELLA But can you, if you would?

ANGELO Look, what I will not, that I cannot do.   (II, 2)

Angelo is incapable of acting inauthentically, of acting contrary to his nature: his integrity is total, in that it makes it impossible for him to falsify himself. But in the context of a society which works by human compromise and half-measure, Angelo's authenticity shows up as frightening and destructive. The tension is the tension of *Troilus* and *Hamlet*: to live in society, a man must be prepared to modify his integrity. Isabella's arguments against Angelo, as we have seen, are ineffective precisely because they are appeals for him to dislocate his private and public selves, to repress his real instincts in the interests of humanity.* She appeals to the concrete, existential circumstances of human life:

> If he had been as you, and you as he,
> You would have slipp'd like him . . .   (II, 2)

---

* Isabella pleads for this dislocation in almost the same terms which in *Troilus* were used to express a rejection of it:
>   O, it is excellent
>   To have a giant's strength! But it is tyrannous
>   To use it like a giant.   (II, 2)
— compare Cressida in *Troilus*: 'They that have the voice of lions and the act of hares, are they not monsters?' (III, 2)

and this echoes Escalus's earlier comment that Angelo himself might easily have fallen, given the chance coming together of circumstances:

Had time coher'd with place, or place with wishing,
Or that the resolute acting of your blood
Could have attain'd th' effect of your own purpose . . .   (II,1)

But the existential position, as always, involves a complete relativism, a lack of constancy: if all men's virtues are simply contingent on time and place, then all evaluation and all consistent identity seem to be cancelled. Angelo sees that society has to work on the basis of consistent, intrinsic values and identities; if men are simply to be valued according to their circumstances, they are fluid, interchangeable. Isabella herself suggests this interchangeability of identity as an instance of the falseness of any absolute stand, as the remark quoted above indicates; but in fact she undermines her own argument:

I would to heaven I had your potency,
And you were Isabel! Should it then be thus?   (II, 2)

The answer to this, by Isabella's own standards, is obviously 'yes': if men are their circumstances and nothing more, which the extreme of the existentialist position would suggest, then to put oneself in someone else's circumstances is to become them: if Isabella were Angelo she would act like him, and condemn Claudio. Angelo sees that this shifting of identities is part of the whole relativism which Isabella's position implies, and which he is concerned to reject; he admits that all men are capable of guilt, including himself, but does not see why this should be made the basis of a disowning of judgement, as long as he himself is ready to undergo the punishments he metes out. His chief wish is to avoid individual particularities of judgement: law must be common and therefore constant, 'and nothing come in partial'.

For wholeness, a man's public and private selves must be in continuity. But *Measure for Measure* also shows that the way a man sees himself and the way he sees others must be adjusted. This is the Gospel resolution of the problem of the self and others: a man must behave towards others as he would have them behave towards himself, as he would behave towards himself: he must be as close to others as he is to himself. In this way others cease to be tools or objects and become subjects, sharing the same life. The extent to which a man shares in the lives of others is reflected in the extent to which he judges them: he must judge others as he would wish himself to be judged. In this way, the reciprocity of condemnation on which Angelo takes his stand can be replaced by the reciprocity of forgiveness.

This is the major criticism of Angelo's ethic: that it involves the kind of circular and ultimately vicious reciprocity of evaluating which we saw in the Greeks in *Troilus*, and in the society of *Hamlet*:

> You may not so extenuate his offence
> For I have had such faults; but rather tell me,
> When I, that censure him, do so offend,
> Let mine own judgment pattern out my death ...   (II,1)

Angelo wants himself to be judged in exactly the same measure to which he gives out judgement, and the process is continuous and enclosed: the man who passes judgement on another is laying down the pattern by

which another will pass judgement on him, and that
other will himself be judged; in the very moment of
condemning another one is condemning oneself. This
is the kind of inter-definition which went on in *Hamlet*,
the condition of all men as simultaneously judged and
judger, subject and object. The process, as Angelo sees
it, is in fact pointless: every man makes his own judgement into an absolute within a closed system of circular
definitions which allows no real constancy at all, no
true absolute. Angelo, in trying to erect an absolute by
asking for his own act of judgement to be taken as final
precisely because he is open to the same kind of judgement himself, is exposing the very flaw of the argument.
The circularity that he offers as a virtue, the reciprocity,
is in fact the very thing wrong with the system: it cancels all absolutes, any hope of a constant criterion. It is
as relative, in its own way, as the individualist, existentialist position of Isabella and Lucio; we remember the
similarity of the relativism of both Greek and Trojan
viewpoints in *Troilus*. If all men share in a community
of guilt, simultaneously condemning and being condemned in a circular process, there is no reason why
this should not be the ground for a community of
forgiveness: all men may forgive each other precisely
because all men are guilty. The only act of judgement
can then be from someone outside the closed system,
not himself open to judgement: for the Christian this
is Christ, in *Measure for Measure* it is the Duke.

The reciprocity of relationships in society, the continual intermeshing of men and actions, is a major
theme in the play, and two chief ideas are used to mirror
this: the idea of marriage, and the idea of changing
identities. The Duke's words to Escalus about Angelo

in his first speech of the play introduce and emphasise the theme of identity:

What figure of us think you he will bear?   (I, 1)

Angelo is not to be an agent of the Duke, a tool to be manipulated, as men in *Hamlet* are manipulated; he is to be both free and responsible, himself yet related: fully autonomous, but answerable to the Duke for his actions. The relationship he stands in to the Duke is in fact very close to the way the Christian conceives of man's relationship to God: man is both himself and God's, fully free yet fully responsible. This is the fusion we have seen already in the way the Duke resigns power to Escalus and Angelo: they are to be him, and he is to be in them, yet he is separate from them, outside the system of which they are part. The relationship of the Duke to Angelo is thus an ideal model of all relationship: Angelo does not resign his selfhood to the Duke, he remains a source, a subject, but his real self now functions in terms of the Duke, to whom he is responsible. The Duke's figure is stamped on Angelo, and therefore he belongs to him as a coin belongs to the sovereign whose image is printed on it. Angelo's relationship to the Duke resembles the relationship between man and Nature as the Duke describes it: a man must simultaneously use his gifts to the full, in free self-expression, while remembering that these gifts are lent to him by a source which will demand a precise account of the expenditure. In the next scene, the image of coin-stamping is re-echoed in Claudio's statement that Julietta carries 'writ' on her the character of their love-making, the child: in the act of love a couple literally make a new person, as the Duke metaphorically re-makes Angelo in his own image in the first scene, and makes him into a married man in Act V Scene 1. Julietta's womb, as Lucio says to Isabella, 'expresseth (Claudio's) full tilth and husbandry': Claudio's act expresses him fully, as Angelo is the complete expression of the Duke. The idea is carried further in Isabella's remark that she and Julietta are mutually adopted cousins: they exchanged names, and thus re-made themselves in the image of each other. To change names mutually is to become two in one, as Angelo bears the Duke's name, and this exchanging of identities, becoming two in one, happens at the deepest level in marriage. Marriage defeats the objectifying circularity of Hamlet's society and the Greek camp: in marriage each is at once himself and the other, treating and judging the other as himself. Marriage is the true and mutual receiving of the print of the other, in contrast to the taking of a false print, which involves exploitation. Isabella sees that Julietta is exploited, when she complains to Angelo that women are 'credulous to false prints', broken, like mirrors, as easily as they make forms.

Reciprocity of characters is imaged throughout in the plot, which makes use constantly of substitution, mistake, disguise, paradox. Substitution is not merely metaphorical but deeply physical, a substitution of heads or bodies: again the central image for this marriage, where the couple are two in one flesh:

PROVOST ... Can you cut off a man's head?

POMPEY If a man be a bachelor, sir, I can; but if he be a married man, he's his wife's head, and I can never cut off a woman's head.   (IV, 2)

It is St Paul's epistles, as with so much else in this play, that are being echoed here, but the immediate echo is from *Hamlet*:

HAMLET ... Farewell, dear mother.

CLAUDIUS Thy loving father, Hamlet.

HAMLET My mother: father and mother is man and wife; man and wife is one flesh; and so, my mother.   (IV, 3)

Hamlet's remark is savage, but it exposes a kind of interrelationship which defeats the condition of exploitation and objectivity the play reveals. In *Measure for Measure*, the union of two in one flesh is a dominant theme: Julietta and Claudio, Angelo and Mariana, Lucio and his bawd, are physically linked in this way, but so too, metaphorically, are Angelo and the Duke, Julietta and Isabella (as children), and the Duke and the Friar. The union of the Duke and the Friar, of a man with himself, reflects the desired union, the relationship which defeats exploitation; the opposite kind of relationship, one in which a man is used as a tool, occurs in the Provost's using of Pompey as assistant to Abhorson, the hangman, which is a 'cash-nexus' affair, a matter of direct need on both sides. Physical kinship is seen, even by those in authority, as the most powerful prohibition of judgement and condemnation: Angelo says he would condemn Claudio 'were he my kinsman, brother or my son', and the Provost declares he would not save Barnadine even if he were his brother. It is impossible to condemn someone who is one flesh with oneself because this is to condemn oneself: full judgement involves making a man an object, placing oneself over against him as a weighing subject, and this cannot be done when two people are 'in' each other,

as Escalus says the Duke is 'in' him (V, 1). A man
cannot fully objectify one who is one flesh with him any
more than he can objectify himself. To be in one flesh
with another is to act towards them as one would act
towards oneself: there is thus no need for cerebral
effort to act well in this condition, action is spontaneously
responsible.

The substitution of Mariana for Isabella images this
interchangeability of bodies, and the image is forced
home with a peculiar insistence on the significance of
knowledge of another. The Duke is a man who has
'ever striven to know himself', and knowledge of self,
for him, involves knowledge of others: a man comes to
know himself as he learns to know others. This is the
process which Angelo must pass through, coming to
self-knowledge through close dealing with others: it is
in communication, relationship, that a man finds himself. Angelo begins in ignorance of himself and others,
and the fact is brought out specifically in his ignorance
of Mariana:

> I have known my husband; yet my husband
> Knows not that ever he knew me.   (V, 1)

Angelo's ignorance of Mariana implies ignorance of
himself: as he does not know she is his wife he does not
know he is her husband. His ignorance also involves
a false knowledge of Isabella, whom he thinks he has
known as a wife:

> Why, just, my lord, and that is Angelo,
> Who thinks he knows that he ne'er knew my body,
> But knows he thinks that he knows Isabel's.   (V, 1)

The complexity of this, the circular, riddle-like quality,

expresses the feeling of the reciprocity of human knowing: it is reminiscent of Thersites's banter with Patroc-
clus in *Troilus* (II, 3), where knowledge of self is again
seen as totally dependent on knowledge of others.
Knowledge must be reciprocal, mutually established,
and the deepest image of this is carnal knowledge.
Angelo is one flesh with Mariana without knowing it,
and this ignorance reflects his general lack of knowledge
of men, the ignorance which made him condemn
Claudio. To judge others harshly is to show a lack of
self-knowledge, because all judgement, in the continuous reciprocity of human society, is judgement of oneself. Angelo fails to see all men are one flesh with each
other, and as a result condemns Claudio.

Reciprocity, again, is the theme of the Duke's conversation with Julietta about her sin with Claudio:

DUKE Love you the man that wronged you?

JULIETTA Yes, as I love the woman that wrong'd him.

DUKE So then, it seems, your most offenceful act was mutually
   committed.   (II, 2)

The sin was mutually committed, and therefore mutual
forgiveness is possible: a community of guilt can lead,
naturally, to a community of forgiveness. Julietta loves
Claudio as she loves herself (as the Friar says he loves the
Duke like himself), and the mutual wronging can be,
also, a mutual loving.

The ending of the play underlines the sense of a
complete reciprocity of selves, a mutual sharing of life
which prohibits total judgement. The prisoner whom
the Provost brings in is 'as like almost to Claudio as
himself', and this closeness is reflected in the Duke's
offer of marriage to Isabella:

What's mine is yours, and what is yours is mine.   (V, 1)

The Duke, by becoming Isabella's husband, will also become one with Claudio, who will then be his brother.

It is in loving knowledge of each other that forgiveness can be established, and the fullest image of forgiveness is therefore marriage, the fullest mutual loving knowledge. To slander and falsify another in speech, as Lucio does, is to show a lack of either love or knowledge or both, as the Duke's rebuke to Lucio indicates:

Lucio Sir, I know him, and I love him.

Duke Love talks with better knowledge, and knowledge with dearer love.   (III, 2)

Love and knowledge are not distinct, contradictory: they grow in proportion to each other. It is this truth which brings us back to the fusion of freedom and exactness, fullness of self-expression and responsibility, which we saw in the Duke's consigning of power to Angelo. *Troilus and Cressida* ends on a note of incompatibility between wisdom and loving, free, spontaneous action and reflective responsibility. It is these poles which *Measure for Measure* can unify, by taking the ideas of love and forgiveness as central. For in both love and forgiveness there is a shifting of the centre of the self which makes responsiveness and responsibility to another natural and spontaneous: one identifies with the other, and knowledge of and care for the other is then as authentically personal as self-knowledge, self-caring. But the fact that identity is not cancelled in love, but shifted, means that this freedom and fullness operates within a specific context of identity and relationship, as Angelo's freedom operates within the defining limits of the Duke's personality.

To love is therefore to act within a particular pattern which is public, epitomised in the public fact of marriage. Love and law must be fused: in a good society it is law which is the living, articulated definition of the limits of wisdom, and to step outside these limits is for men to be less than themselves, less than authentic. This is so, clearly, only if the law is truly humane, not external to human experience but responsive to it: love and knowledge are unified when men are authentically lawful, when the law is in their hearts and tongues, and good action therefore spontaneous. In this condition, the law will both create and define the limits of human authenticity and grow from this authenticity: men must not merely authenticate external restraints – an action which can make tyranny easy – but by drawing the law into their personal experience must make it humane, in a reciprocal movement. Responsibility can then become real freedom, creative bondage: the Duke, when going to minister to the Provost's prisoners, says he goes 'bound by his charity', and it is this fusion of defined limits and free self-giving that the play is exploring.

So love and forgiveness in the play are not intangible feelings beyond the public world, but move within a precision of form, within particular designs and relationships. One consistent theme in the play is the idea of a fusion of pure spontaneity and complex thinking, the polarities of *Troilus* and *Hamlet*. This is brought out in a specific way by the recurring sense of a constant, growing design which maintains its singleness of purpose and spontaneous life through all the complexities of its working. The idea of carrying through a design with constancy, not allowing it to be deflected, is there in the Duke's command to Escalus not to 'warp' from the commission he has been given; it is the idea, too, behind the continual prevarications of Pompey in Act II Scene 3. Pompey tells his story in a muddled way, branching off onto side-themes and losing track of the main point, and Escalus has to call him back 'to the purpose'. Later on, Angelo instructs the Provost through a messenger to carry out his plan exactly, and not to 'swerve from the smallest article of it' (IV, 2).

Pompey's lack of coherent pattern contrasts with the Duke's conception of a whole design, which he controls and fosters throughout the play, without letting it be deflected at any point. The unity of the Duke's design comes through forcibly when he outlines to Isabella his plot to trap Angelo:

> . . . Therefore fasten your ear on my advisings; to the love I have in doing good a remedy presents itself. I do make myself believe that you may most uprighteously do a poor wronged lady a merited benefit; redeem your brother from the angry law; do no stain to your own gracious person; and much please the absent Duke, if peradventure he shall ever return to have hearing of this business.   (III, 1)

A single action will simultaneously achieve all these aims; the complexity of the plot is contained and controlled within it. The design, unlike the design of the Greeks in *Troilus*, propels itself through the complexities without being strangled by them: spontaneity and complex thought are held in perfect fusion. The image used of the Duke's design is one of organic, spontaneous growth: Isabella trusts that his plan 'will grow to a most prosperous perfection' and the 'unfolding star' which the Duke sees in the sky when he has disclosed his plan to Isabella is a minor image of this natural process.

The Duke's words to Friar Peter also express the sense of a necessary fusion of spontaneous unfolding and inevitable complexity:

> The Provost knows our purpose and our plot.
> The matter being afoot, keep your instruction
> And hold you ever to our special drift;
> Though sometimes you do blench from this to that
> As cause doth minister . . .   (IV, 5)

What is needed, according to the Duke, is a constancy of purpose which is not too rigid to cope empirically with specific circumstances: a synthesis of absolute principle and situation-ethics, precision and flexibility. This, again, is the synthesis we have already examined, between the absolute constancy of an Angelo and the existential ethic of Isabella, between unthinking, uncompromising authenticity and an accommodating awareness of actual situations. The opposition of constancy and opportunism is an important theme in the play: Lucio suggests the idea of constancy with his remark to the First Gentleman that 'grace is grace, in spite of all controversy', and this is echoed in Isabella's declaration to the Duke that 'truth is truth to the end of reck'ning'. The Provost is described by the Duke as 'constant'; the Duke 'constantly' believes Mariana; Elbow puts emphasis on the word 'continue', and Mistress Overdone is described by the Provost as a 'a bawd of eleven years continuance'. When Claudio is telling Lucio of Isabella's powers of persuasion, he describes them in terms of both an innate, constant quality, and a specific art:

> . . . for in her youth
> There is a prone and speechless dialect

Such as move men; beside, she hath prosperous art
When she will play with reason and discourse,
And well she can persuade.   (I, 2)

Craft and ignorance are alike in that they both fall short
of the synthesis of spontaneity and complexity. Angelo's
spontaneity, his complete truth-to-self, is based on ignorance: his ability to be purely himself is in inverse
proportion to his compassionate understanding of
others, of actual living. He is as Lucio describes the
First Gentleman – not healthy, but 'so sound as things
that are hollow'. Lucio, on the other hand, has no integrity, only craft, a tactical ability without constancy:
he refuses to stand bail for a friend. Craft and ignorance are thus connected, as similar kinds of failure: the
Duke tells Lucio, when he is slandering him, that he
is speaking either unskilfully or craftily; Angelo thinks
that the pleading Isabella is either ignorant, or craftily
pretending to be. When Angelo falls from the position
of pure (if hollow) authenticity, he becomes totally
emmeshed in tactics, cunning:

Alack, when once our grace we have forgot,
Nothing goes right; we would, and we would not.   (IV, 4)

His former integrity of self is shattered, diffused, as his
thoughts and prayers are: he thinks and prays in fragments, to 'several subjects'. He loses that spontaneity
which came from complete integrity of self, from constancy of purpose, and surrenders himself up to plotting.

The Duke's plotting, in contrast to Angelo's, is
strategic, not tactical. He has conceived a whole, organic
design, a single action, to develop which he becomes
involved in the tactics of the moment. But always,

behind the tactics, is the larger design, sustaining and directing. The Duke's life is a living fusion of spontaneity, organic development, and that reflective responsiveness to actual needs and demands which is the basis of social responsibility. To use a phrase of Dr Leavis's in a quite different context, he is an example of 'spontaneity supervening on complex development'.*

The two dominant themes of the last Act, marriage and forgiveness, both show in similar ways this interpenetration of freedom and precision, mercy and justice, spontaneity and social responsibility. The Duke forgives Angelo and Lucio, but he is a severe man too, as his earlier advocacy of strict punishment for Pompey indicates. Within the context of forgiveness, a weighing and balancing, a giving of measure for measure, takes place. Forgiveness is a free, gratuitous act, one cutting behind the received valuations, a generous giving of mercy in a place where, by absolute standards, it is undeserved, but the valuations and weighings have still to be made, before forgiveness takes place. In this way, what the Duke achieves in his act of both giving measure for measure and forgiving is a fusion of the two opposed ethics of the Greeks and Trojans in *Troilus*. Forgiveness is a personal creation of value, a free and spontaneous giving of love, regardless of intrinsic worth and merit; justice, on the other hand, works on the basis of balanced proportions, action and reaction. The Duke manages to do both: he gives people in marriage to those they deserve, but also forgives, cancels out offences.

---

* Cf. *Revaluation*, Chatto and Windus, 1936, p. 170; the phrase is used about Wordsworth.

Marriage, too, is an image of this kind of fusion. Marriage depends on certain intrinsic fitnesses, as the Duke makes clear: it is a matter of justice that Angelo and Mariana, Lucio and his bawd, should accept each other. But marriage, also, is basically a gratuitous commitment, precisely because, like forgiveness, it is total, permanent and unconditional: for the Christian, it is a transcendental act in the sense that it creates a constant reality, one which will continue independently of what actually happens in specific terms to the people concerned. Marriage is therefore both absolute, constant, gratuitous, and a matter of intrinsic fitnesses and compatibilities; in this way it resembles forgiveness. Again, marriage, as we have seen, is the public sanctioning of personal passion, the linking of personal, authentic life with society, making this life socially responsible without diminishing its authenticity. So in this sense as well marriage serves as an image of the synthesis which the play struggles towards.

The idea of death, as it occurs in the play, is also relevant to the themes we have been tracing. Death is similar to the judgement of the law in the sense that all men must undergo it, regardless of personal choice; like law, too, it levels all values, 'makes these odds all even', as the Duke says to Claudio. All men must undergo death, but there are two possible attitudes to be taken towards it: men can either fight it, resenting it as a regrettable necessity, or they can make it their own in an act of total acceptance, as Claudio declares he will do:

> If I must die,
> I will encounter darkness as a bride
> And hug it in mine arms.   (III, 1)

Barnadine, on the other hand, refuses to accept his death: he is 'unfit to live or die', and rather than force him unwillingly to the block, the Duke asks for time to 'persuade this rude wretch willingly to die' (IV, 3). Death, like the law, must be personally authenticated: Claudio, previously unwilling to accept death, is convinced by the Duke's persuasion and learns to embrace the fact of death, to desire what is inevitable. His ability to do this is an advance over his attitude of mind when arrested: then he saw his individual experience as the dominant reality, and the law as an external restraint; he begins by seeing death similarly, but then finds that, by assimilating the fact of death, he can live without fear. Attitudes towards death are therefore an extension of attitudes towards the law: in both cases men are faced with a force beyond them, restricting their individual freedom, and in both cases it is by authenticating the force, making it part of their personal life, that the problem can be solved.

But it would be wrong to turn completely to the fact of death, as a way of avoiding involvement in actual, living situations. This is a tempting position, because it can give a kind of constancy of self, a fixed absolute, beyond the shifting complexity of life. But this constancy, gained only by a rejection of commitment to life, is a false one, as Angelo's constancy is merely the result of his ignorance of actual living. This is the position of Barnadine: Barnadine is totally disengaged from life, passively accepting his imprisonment, careless of everything, and this stance has an attractive integrity about it. Like Achilles in *Troilus*, Barnadine is fully and constantly himself, without swerving a hair in concession to others or to circumstance. Beside this

ultimate disengagement, all human involvements can
be made to appear futile and ridiculous, as Achilles
makes the plans of the Greeks look foolish. The Duke
offers this attitude to Claudio, arguing that life can be
seen for the absurd, tactical affair it is once the uncompromising absolutism of death is grasped:

> Be absolute for death; either death or life
> Shall thereby be the sweeter. Reason thus with life.
> If I do lose thee, I do lose a thing
> That none but fools would keep. A breath thou art,
> Servile to all the skyey influences,
> That dost this habitation where thou keep'st
> Hourly afflict . . .   III, 1)

But this kind of absolutism, at its extreme, is an imma-
ture response to the problem, a collapsing of the effort
towards the fusion of constancy and complexity. The
complexity of life must be encountered and engaged
with within the context of a constant, absolute integrity
of the kind that the thought of death can give. But the
two must be held in fusion: to settle entirely for the
absolutism of death, or for the complexity of life, is to
lose sight of real wholeness.

Measure for Measure is about the need to make law
personally authentic, so that spontaneous action may
also be responsible action. But although much of the
play is about the difficulty of making this fusion, it also
becomes clear that there is a deep sense in which law
and experience are already intimately bound up in a
single process before the struggle for synthesis begins.
This sense is expressed in the recurrence of processes
in which good and evil involve each other, of paradoxes
and entanglements of the two. This is there strongly in
Angelo's soliloquy after he is first attracted to Isabella:

Is this her fault or mine?
The tempter or the tempted, who sins most?
Ha!
Not she; nor doth she tempt; but it is I
That, lying by the violet in the sun,
Corrupt with virtuous season. . . .
O cunning enemy, that, to catch a saint,
With saints dost bait thy hook! Most dangerous
Is that temptation which doth goad us on
To sin in loving virtue . . . (II, 2)

This kind of image is frequent in the play: the sense is of a self-defeating process, of a good which creates evil in proportion to its own strength, so that the deeper the good, the deeper the evil. Angelo tells Isabella that her blushes 'banish what they sue for'; before she comes for her second interview with him, he feels the blood muster to his heart in a way which actually deprives him of strength, and he compares this condition to that of a crowd whose pressing attentions only stifle a fainting man further. The Duke says that Angelo's cruelty to Mariana has only increased her love for him, as an impediment in a current makes it more violent: here the process is reversed, and evil creates good in proportion to its own force. When the Duke talks in disguise to Escalus about the state of the world, he declares that 'there is so great a fever on goodness that the dissolution of it must cure it' (III, 2).

Part of the significance of this process seems to lie in the influence of Paul's epistles on the play. Paul sees the law, not only as a restraint on goodness, but as an actual cause of sin: no man will be justified in God's sight by works of the law, since through the law comes knowledge of sin: where there is no law, there can be no transgression. So law is at once a symbol of good and a creator of evil: the fact that it exists means that it can, and will, be broken. This is at the root of Angelo's condition: it is the very purity of Isabella which causes his lust. Good and evil are intertwined, interfeeding, as the law creates the very passions it exists to curb; in this sense there is already a deep relation between law and passion in the actual texture of human life.

This is not, of course, the play's chief discovery. The movement of *Measure for Measure* is the effort to convert this destructive, negative relation of law and passion into a positive synthesis, and in doing so to create a fusion, at least theoretically, of the polarities which dominate the problem plays. To see this fusion more fully developed, we must look at the Last Comedies; but before that, it is necessary to examine the Roman Plays.

CHAPTER FOUR

Coriolanus and *Antony and Cleopatra*

IN the first scene of *Coriolanus*, the patrician Menenius Agrippa points out to the rebellious citizens that their intended violence against the state is futile:

MENENIUS Why, masters, my good friends, mine honest
    neighbours,
Will you undo yourselves?

FIRST CITIZEN We cannot, sir; we are undone already.

MENENIUS I tell you, friends, most charitable care
    Have the patricians of you. For your wants,
    Your suffering in this dearth, you may as well
    Strike at the heaven with your staves as lift them
    Against the Roman state; whose course will on
    The way it takes, cracking ten thousand curbs
    Of more strong link asunder than can ever
    Appear in your impediment. For the dearth,
    The gods, not the patricians, make it, and
    Your knees to them, not arms, must help. Alack,
    You are transported by calamity
    Thither where more attends you . . .   (I, 1)

The theme of this exchange is futility, but the futility takes different forms. The citizen's reply to Menenius's question suggests one kind of pointlessness: the people cannot undo themselves by the violence they are about to commit because they are already undone, at an extreme. The implication behind the citizen's retort is that they have reached a point where they can only improve, not worsen, their condition, where any action will be valuable. To be completely desperate is to have a kind of strength; it can mean that any action is a way forward. To be in this situation is to disturb conventional valuations of the qualities of actions: if any action, is a way forward then all actions are the same, and any choice is gratuitous: what becomes important is the action itself, rather than its results. Mob-violence is presented in the play as precisely this kind of action totally disproportionate to its motivations or results and therefore in a sense self-sustaining, done for its own sake. The people's desperation is focussed sharply in the challenge of the first citizen to the rest as the play opens:

> You are all resolv'd rather to die than to famish?

The offered alternatives here give in fact no alternative at all: either way, ironically, the outcome will be death.

Menenius's speech suggests two kinds of pointless action. He sees the crowd's violence as purposeless primarily because it implies an ability to control what is in fact uncontrollable, the state; to attempt to strike at the state is as futile as trying to strike at heaven. But the futility of this is intensified by the fact that to make the attempt is actively to worsen the situation, to damage it further in the process of trying to improve it. The people's action will be purposeless not only because its success is impossible but because it is self-defeating: it will carry them from the calamity they are in already into greater disaster. Menenius's speech is intended to show the citizens that any action at all on their part is bound to be hopeless: as plebians they are passive elements of society, quite alienated from control over it. Menenius and the citizens thus have opposed views on the significance of plebian action, but paradoxically the views are close in feeling to each other: Menenius sees their action as pointless because it is self-defeating, the citizens acknowledge that their action may be pointless in its specific aims but the futility indicates the value: anything is better than nothing.

Action which is self-defeating or self-consuming is a constant theme in the play. Coriolanus's first words to the citizens emphasise the self-defeating quality of their condition which Menenius suggested:

> What's the matter, you dissentious rogues
> That, rubbing the poor itch of your opinion,
> Make yourselves scabs?   (I, 1)

For Coriolanus, the more the citizens agitate, the more they fester; he goes on to compare their affections to the appetite of a sick man, who most desires that which would make his condition worse. If the senate did not keep order, the citizens would 'feed on one another'. Coriolanus's objection to granting the people any power at all is that it will give them a basis for claiming more power later, in a cumulative and circular process:

> Five tribunes, to defend their vulgar wisdoms,
> Of their own choice . . .
>   . . . 'Sdeath!
> The rabble should have first unroof'd the city
> Ere so prevail'd with me; it will in time
> Win upon power and throw forth greater themes
> For insurrection's arguing.   (I, 1)

He sees the granting of power to the people both as starting a self-consuming process in them – increasing their appetite in proportion to what they get – and as a self-defeating act on the part of the patricians: in appeasing the plebians the patricians are preparing their own downfall:

In soothing them we nourish 'gainst our Senate
The cockle of rebellion, insolence, sedition,
Which we ourselves have plough'd for, sow'd, and scatter'd. . .
    (III, 1)

Self-defeating action, again, is the subject of Valeria's admiring description of young Marcus:

O' my word, the father's son! I'll swear 'tis a very pretty boy. O' my troth, I look'd upon him a Wednesday half an hour together; has such a confirm'd countenance! I saw him run after a gilded butterfly; and when he caught it he let it go again, and after it again, and over and over he comes, and up again, catch'd it again; or whether his fall enrag'd him, or how 'twas, he did so set his teeth and tear it.   (I, 3)

Young Marcus catches and releases the butterfly, not for any specific purpose, but simply to enjoy the activity it involves, activity which ends in sudden, apparently unmotivated destruction. Marcus's activity is circular, self-justifying: he catches the butterfly so he can release it, and releases it so he can catch it. The movement reflects in a minor way the larger pattern of circular activity in the play: the Volscians, defeated in Act I by the Romans, are preparing for another attack at the beginning of Act III. As Coriolanus says, they 'stand but as at first', and the situation is back where it was to begin with. Virgilia's refusal to go out visiting with

Volumnia and Valeria has a similar pointlessness, as Valeria sees:

You would be another Penelope; yet they say all the yarn she spun in Ulysses' absence did but fill Ithaca full of moths. (I, 3).

But the main image of self-defeating action in the play is Coriolanus himself. When Titus Lartius warns him during the battle at Corioli that he is not fit to continue fighting, Coriolanus replies:

My work hath not yet warm'd me. Fare you well;
The blood I drop is rather physical
Than dangerous to me.   (I, 5)

The more blood he sheds, the stronger he grows; the more he acts, the greater his appetite for action becomes. He is warmed by his own work both physically, and in the sense of being warmed to further work, further expenditure of energy. He feeds off his own blood, and is therefore completely self-sufficient, drawing his life only from himself.* It is the realisation that Coriolanus acts for himself, not primarily for the state, which makes the first citizen suspicious of him in the opening scene of the play:

I say unto you, what he hath done famously he did it to that end; though soft-conscienc'd men can be content to say it was for his country, he did it to please his mother and to be partly proud, which he is, even to the altitude of his virtue.   (I, 1)

---

* This self-devouring suggests a kind of cannibalism which is made explicit in the conversation of the two servants of Aufidius when Coriolanus visits the latter's house: the first servant remarks that Coriolanus has inflicted a good deal of punishment on their master, to which the second servant replies: 'An he had been cannibally given, he might have broil'd and eaten him too'   (IV, 5).

The first citizen sees Coriolanus very much as Coriolanus sees the people, as self-consuming: he acts for
his own sake, in a circular process. When the Roman
forces flee from Corioli, Coriolanus prays that they will
be afflicted with boils and plagues, and 'one infect
another/Against the wind a mile'; this is how he sees
the people, as mutually infecting, caught up in an
enclosed process of self-destruction. But a few lines
later his anger drives him to a similar self-consuming:

> Mend and charge home,
> Or, by the fires of heaven, I'll leave the foe
> And make my wars on you.   (I, 4)

He is as ready to turn against his own men as he is to
fight the enemy; the self-defeating quality he detests in
the plebians is there, deeply, in his own instinctive
behaviour. His conflict with the people, as Menenius
sees, is itself a kind of self-devouring, Rome turning
on herself; for Menenius, the people and Coriolanus
share the same life, and for them to fight each other is
monstrous:

> Now the good gods forbid
> That our renowned Rome, whose gratitude
> Towards her deserved children is enroll'd
> In Jove's own book, like an unnatural dam
> Should now eat up her own!   (III, 1)

Menenius and Coriolanus see civil conflict quite
differently; Menenius sees Rome as an organic society
whose health depends on mutual interaction between
patricians and plebians; this is the significance of his
fable of the belly in Act I Scene 1. He envisages a
living, dynamic reciprocity of active and passive

functions as the ideal relationship between rulers and ruled: the belly is passive, yet sends out what it receives to the members; the limbs and organs are active in the sense of performing actions, but are passively dependent for their life on the belly. This relation comes alive when Coriolanus is called on to stand before the people and solicit their voices: the rulers must win the active sanction of those they will rule, and the people refuse to be submissive to any ruler whose role they have not personally authenticated by questioning and decision. Coriolanus himself envisages no reciprocity: he sees this mutual interrelationship of plebians and patricians as circular, destructive, self-defeating. He asks for the people's voices, but, as Sicinius foretells,

> He will require them
> As if he did contemn what he requested
> Should be in them to give.   (II, 2)

But his contempt for the people is, ironically, part of his own self-consuming quality: he rejects the idea that his own actions need any verification outside themselves. To see his actions as responsible to the people destroys for him their purity, their wholeness as things done for themselves, non-referential:

> To brag unto them 'Thus I did, and thus!'
> Show them th'unaching scars which I should hide,
> As if I had receiv'd them for the hire
> Of their breath only!   (II, 2)

In the light of this, the real meaning of Coriolanus's 'pride' becomes clear. His pride, like Achilles's in *Troilus and Cressida*, is a self-creation without reference to society, a self-conferment of value, and it is because it rejects the need for social verification, the evaluations of others, that it is enclosed and therefore self-consuming. Coriolanus is a man of massive integrity, wholly authentic; but his authenticity consists in keeping himself clear of the defining evaluations of his society, preserving a personal wholeness which social communication and responsibility can, to him, only dilute. He is fully alive in the process of acting, most himself when on the battlefield; to return from there to the city is to return from the pleasure of self-definition to the irrelevancies of public response and demand. His personal actions grow out of his control and raise complex social consequences which he can ignore but not finally evade, which threaten his private wholeness.

Coriolanus is obsessed with truth, but truth as authenticity, not loyalty or fidelity. The two meanings of truth, truth-to-self and truth-to-others, are dislocated in him: it is his nature to be wholly himself, and he stays committed to this wholeness even when it involves betraying others, turning on his own society. In Coriolanus, authentic self-expression and social responsibility are not merely maladjusted but totally at odds, intrinsically incompatible: the kind of complex responsiveness to others, to situations, which social responsibility involves, eats into the massive, single-tracked constancy which authentic living implies, deflecting spontaneity into compromising tactics. Coriolanus's attitude to truth is brought out in significant contrast to Cominius's, in the battle scenes of Act I: Cominius is met by a messenger bringing bad news of the Roman army, and replies to the man's announcement:

> Though thou speak'st truth,
> Methinks thou speak'st not well.   (I, 6)

When Coriolanus appears and corrects the messenger's news, Cominius is ready to beat the man, but Coriolanus stops him:

> Let him alone;
> He did inform the truth.   (I, 6)

For Coriolanus, truth is a value in itself, worthy of admiration: it is the truth of the messenger's news which he sees, not the quality or significance of the content. For Cominius it is the quality of the content, not the fact of truth, which is most important: he looks at truth, not as an isolated value in itself, but in the context of its substance, unwilling to detach the authentic quality of the messenger's report from the nature and consequences of the message itself. Coriolanus sees truth as an absolute criterion, regardless of the circumstances of it; when he tells Aufidius that he hates him 'worse than a promise-breaker' he is putting him beyond his ultimate term of abuse – and again it is a term which slides over the nature of the promise involved.

It is truth-to-self regardless of human context which characterises Coriolanus. He is concerned that his action should be authentic, not that it should be responsible, and the crux of the play is that he is brought to the point of decision between the two. Authenticity and social responsibility have in fact coincided for much of his career, which is why many of the people in the play miss the truth of his nature: his personal self-definition in military activity has happened also to be useful to his society. But it is coincidence, and not fusion, which is the significant term: Coriolanus fights, not primarily for his society, but for himself; like

Troilus, he uses a public event, the war, as material for self-definition. His attitude to the war is irresponsible: he cannot understand the tactic of withdrawal to achieve a positive purpose, as Cominius practises it: he asks, impatiently, why Cominius's troops have stopped fighting. He himself is in perpetual activity, like a machine; having finished one battle he goes on immediately to another. When he hears that the Volscians are in arms, his response is one of pleasure at an opportunity for action, not concern for his society: the Volscian attack will give the Romans a chance to 'vent (their) musty superfluity'. The question of whether the Roman army has met the Volscians becomes the material for a private wager between himself and Titus Lartius at the beginning of Act I Scene 4. His relationship with Aufidius is merely a private rivalry:

> Were half to half the world by th' ears, and he
> Upon my party, I'd revolt, to make
> Only my wars with him.   (I, 1)

It is because Coriolanus sees military action as self-definition that he is uninterested in the response of Roman society to his achievements. Cominius, seeing that Coriolanus is shrugging off his countrymen's praises, warns him not to become 'the grave of (his) deserving': the image captures the self-concealing, self-destroying quality of any action not available for public verification. To conceal his actions from others, says Cominius, would be worse than theft. Coriolanus replies that his wounds 'smart to hear themselves rememb'red', and refuses to take a 'bribe' for his exploits; his actions are done, past, and because it is acting itself which concerns him, he has no interest in their social consequences. Cominius rejects Coriolanus's self-belittling and says that he must be forced, if necessary, to accept the city's own evaluation:

> Too modest are you;
> More cruel to your good report than grateful
> To us that give you truly. By your patience,
> If 'gainst yourself you be incens'd, we'll put you—
> Like one that means his proper harm—in manacles,
> Then reason safely with you.   (I, 9)

Coriolanus rejects the evaluations of others, but it is these which 'give' him truly: Cominius sees that he is unable to judge himself, as, in a different context, Menenius realises that if Brutus and Sicinius were able to 'turn (their) eyes towards the napes of (their) necks', they would see themselves truly, as he sees them. Coriolanus refuses to allow that action is public, a personal self-disclosure to society, and thus refuses public evaluations; he must be manacled before he will hear reason, and the state of being manacled emphasises the self-enclosed condition of this individualism. Cominius's comment on Coriolanus's modesty confirms the fact that his 'pride' has nothing to do with wanting glory in other men's eyes, but is the exact opposite, a rejection of any element of social consideration in action.

Later, in describing Coriolanus's behaviour at Corioli, Cominius exposes his individualism in terms which re-echo *Troilus and Cressida*:

> Our spoils he kick'd at,
> And look'd upon things precious as they were
> The common muck of the world. He covets less

Than misery itself would give, *rewards*
His deeds with doing them, and is content
To spend the time to end it. (II, 2)

Coriolanus rejects common, received valuations, and
the rejection is closely related to a circularity of action,
action done as its own reward and its own purpose: to
reject conventional valuations is to reject conventional
motives and ends. He hates the idea of his deeds being
publicly discussed, and leaves the Capitol before
Cominius gives an account of them; he says he would
rather have his wounds over again than hear how he
got them. He sees the very act of social communication as falsifying, mere reportage and flattery as against
the authentic reality of actions:

I had rather have one scratch my head i' th' sun
When the alarum were struck than idly sit
To hear my nothings *monster'd.* (II, 2)

The denial of public communication is a denial of self-
giving, an enclosedness: he refuses to show his scars
in public to the people but suggests, half-ironically,
that he will reveal them in private. The act of communication which is asked of him, in confronting the
people and submitting to their inquiry, is an image of
the balanced reciprocity of a personal relationship, a
mutual giving and submitting and verifying. Coriolanus refuses even for a moment to become an object,
even when this is in order to be a subject, ruler of the
people; by failing to see that relationship must involve
a reciprocity of subject and object, each submitting to
the other to be free, he rejects the possibility of relationship altogether. He behaves throughout

> As if a man were author of himself
> And knew no other kin.   (V, 3)

When he goes over to the Volscians and turns on Rome, he rejects the name which Rome has publicly and ceremonially given him:

> 'Coriolanus'
> He would not answer to; forbad all names;
> He was a kind of nothing, titleless,
> Till he had forg'd himself a name i' th' fire
> Of burning Rome.   (V, 1)

He refuses names as he refuses speech, as part of a public communication not only superfluous but distorting; he creates himself in action, forging a name and identity for himself, refusing the offered definitions of others. He is a totally self-created man, who, as Sicinius says, 'easily endures not article/Tying him to aught' (II, 3). The importance of speech, as an act of self-communication in which a man is available to others, is insistently present in the scenes of Coriolanus's encounter with the people as candidate for consul, and the whole dramatic tension of these scenes grows from the incongruity between the physical easiness of speech and the deep complexity of its consequences. It is the sheer act of asking for the people's voices which is sufficient to establish communication between Coriolanus and the citizens: he has only to articulate the necessary formula. The first citizen makes this clear in his answer to Coriolanus's sneering inquiry as to the price of consulship: 'The price is to ask it kindly'. But the consequences of the simple act are deeply social, and it is the claims of this responsibility which Coriolanus rejects, in refusing to commit him-

self to others. His reluctance to make the simple request demanded of him contrasts with his readiness to
use language to exploit the citizens:

> I will, sir, flatter my sworn brother, the people, to earn a
> dearer estimation of them; 'tis a condition they account gentle;
> and since the wisdom of their choice is rather to have my hat
> than my heart, I will practise the insinuating nod and be off to
> them most counterfeitly.   (II, 3)

The affected elegance of this is intended to confuse the
uneducated citizens, as Hamlet's obscure speech
exploits his hearers: language is turned against itself,
used to avoid, rather than to establish, communication.

It is because Coriolanus is committed only to his
own wholeness that his action in deserting Rome and
fighting against it with his previous enemies is completely logical. When he is unable to be himself any
longer in Rome, hindered by the demands of social
responsibility, he turns for his self-fulfilment to Corioli.
The logic of this is mirrored in the logic of his relationship with Aufidius changing from one of deadly rivalry
to one of loving union. The relationship was in fact a
kind of love-relationship all along, an intense personal
encounter excluding the world or transforming the
world within itself, like the relationship of Antony and
Cleopatra. Like that relationship, too, love and hatred
lie close together, and one can slide into the other:

> Let me twine
> Mine arms about that body, where against
> My grained ash an hundred times hath broke
> And scarr'd the moon with splinters; here I clip
> The anvil of my sword, and do contest

As hotly and as nobly with thy love
As ever in ambitious strength I did
Contend against thy valour.   (IV, 5)

The ease with which the relationship of Coriolanus and
Aufidius moves from hostility to affection comes from
the fact that, in both cases, the relationship exists in a
vacuum; it is shaped, not by social or political considerations, but simply by its own energy, and because it is
closed to factors outside itself it can remain intact in
spite of a whole change of circumstances. This is
Coriolanus's personal condition: he remains constant
in his pursuit of self-definition wherever he is, whatever
side he is on. Aufidius's remark to one of his soldiers
after the Volscian defeat epitomises this complete lack
of relationship with a society, a lack both leaders share:

I would I were a Roman; for I cannot,
Being a Volsce, be that I am.   (I, 10)

Aufidius does not see his identity as bound up with his
society, his personal action in terms of a community;
on the contrary, he sees his society as contradicting his
identity, defining him falsely. To be part of a defeated
city is to be untrue to his 'real' self, which is undefeated,
victorious: his real self is thus an absolute, unchanging
principle, untouched by the flux of actual circumstance,
staying true to itself in spite of its context. Coriolanus
is basically no more a Roman than Aufidius is a Volscian;
he is a Roman when the circumstances of the city
correspond with his own sense of himself, and he leaves
Rome when the two conflict. He is a constant force,
self-verifying, without need of social definition; he
refuses even the degree of social control over his life

involved in being banished, and reverses the relationship with a magnificent gesture, asserting himself as a
subject and objectifying the whole city: 'I banish
you'.

The paradox of Coriolanus is exposed in the action
of the play: he is a traitor whose whole life centres
round his integrity, a man who through commitment
to himself is divided against his own flesh and blood.
Twice in the play his commitment to himself and to
others are tragically incompatible: by refusing politic
compromise and self-falsification, he turns on his
family and his city; in turning back to his own flesh and
blood, to his wife and mother and son, he condemns
himself at the hands of the Volscians. Aufidius's reply to
the first conspirator's inquiry about Coriolanus suggests
this self-devouring: Coriolanus, he says, fares

> As with a man by his own alms empoison'd,
> And with his charity slain.   (V, 6)

The man whose action was self-sustaining, closed off
from others and performed for its own sake, is killed,
ironically, as a result of the only act of love and mercy
he does: this, too, is self-destroying.

*   *   *

Coriolanus is about the conflict of authentic life and
social responsibility, the tension between the way a man
conceives of himself and the social character which is
offered for him to make his own. Coriolanus is wholly
authentic, but his authenticity can exist only outside
society; for him, any demand or action coming from
outside himself is inauthentic, to be rejected. When he

is brought before the people in the white gown of humility, he is being asked to choose between integrity and responsibility, between his spontaneous impulses and the demands, traditional and actual, of a whole society. But this cannot in any sense be seen as a straight fight between two kinds of positive value; neither value is acceptable in itself as the play presents them, simply because they are presented as separate alternatives. Coriolanus's integrity, like Angelo's in *Measure for Measure*, is a false integrity, false precisely because it excludes responsibility to others, and can maintain itself only by this exclusion: responsibility, faced with this uncompromising constancy, can and does degenerate into opportunism, unprincipled tactics.

The issue can be seen, as in *Measure for Measure*, as a conflict betwen constancy and fickleness, absolutism and situation-ethics. To put it this way is in itself to focus the tension: an admirable and vital constancy can be seen also as a hard, unresponsive absolutism; a complex, reflective situation-ethics, flexible enough to deal with actual crises of human responsibility, can be from another viewpoint a merely existential response to circumstances which cancels consistent values and spills over into expediency. The dangers of absolutism are exposed in Menenius's description to the people of the Roman state: it is a force

> . . . whose course will on
> The way it takes, cracking ten thousand curbs
> Of more strong link asunder than can ever
> Appear in your impediment.   (I, 1)

In trying to demonstrate the constancy and stability of the state, Menenius succeeds merely in revealing its failure; the state is a blind force, totally unresponsive to the needs and demands of the people it exists to protect, forging a single course through the complexities of human circumstance, fulfilling its own purposes in disconnection from those of the citizens. The comparison with Coriolanus is evident:

> His sword, death's stamp,
> Where it did mark, it took; from face to foot
> He was a thing of blood, whose every motion
> Was tim'd with dying cries. Alone he ent'red
> The mortal gate of th' city, which he painted
> With shunless destiny; aidless came off,
> And with a sudden re-enforcement struck
> Corioli like a planet.   (II, 2)

The blind, autonomous motion of the Roman state becomes the quality of Coriolanus's personal activity; he is a 'thing', himself 'shunless' in the mechanical inevitability of his action, moving with a precise rhythm (his motion is 'tim'd' with dying cries). But it is the precision which hints at the potential value of this state of being. For this description of Coriolanus in battle can be seen as a kind of grotesque caricature of a spontaneity of action which, without the hard unresponsiveness of this mechanical motion, is valuable. There is no dislocation at all between purpose and action in Coriolanus's activity, and this continuity is imaged in the accuracy of his sword: 'where it did mark, it took'. The spontaneity is part of his integrity: he *is* his actions, without falsification, his actions are precise and perfect self-expressions. In the descriptions of both Coriolanus and the Roman state, the callous inflexibility is ironically close to the kind of spontaneity which, for Shakespeare, human action must achieve if it is to be authentically self-expressive; the problem, as with Angelo, is how to prevent spontaneity from being a ruthless, disruptive force. A man who can only be himself will prove too intense for a society which has to live by politic compromise, by exchanging a degree of self-falsification for a degree of peace.

It is essential to see in the play how the tension involved in this closeness of inhuman autonomy to total integrity is preserved by a delicate balancing of responses to Coriolanus himself, and to his enemies. The image of the undeviating Roman state which Menenius uses in addressing the citizens is echoed later in Coriolanus's angry accusation of Sicinius, the people's tribune: Sicinius, he tells the senators, is a man who

> . . . wants not spirit
> To say he'll turn your current in a ditch,
> And make your channel his.   (III, 1)

Here an image previously used to suggest cruel absolutism becomes, when opposed to the manœuvring of Sicinius, an image of spontaneous constancy; a man who resembles a one-track current may be dangerous, but he has at least a kind of integrity lacking in those who cunningly divert the energies and purposes of others for their own ends.

Coriolanus's authenticity is emphasised constantly in the play. He is a man who cannot help but be himself, a man with a massive singleness of identity; his early remark about Aufidius is the nearest he ever gets to imagining himself as something different from what he is, to seeing himself and another as even remotely interchangeable:

> I sin in envying his nobility;
> And were I anything but what I am,
> I would wish me only he.   (I, 1)

Menenius sees Coriolanus's authenticity as a matter of identity between his heart and tongue:

> His heart's his mouth;
> What his breast forges, that his tongue must vent. . .   (III, 1)

and these are the terms in which Volumnia appeals to him to compromise for the sake of Rome; she begs him to speak,

> . . . not by your own instruction,
> Nor by th' matter which your heart prompts you,
> But with such words that are but roted in
> Your tongue, though but bastards and syllables
> Of no allowance to your bosom's truth.   (III, 2)

She is asking him to make a complete dislocation between his private and public selves, so complete that he can safely disregard the words he speaks as of no significance at all.* Coriolanus sets his own constancy against the fickleness of the people, in his first speech:

---

* Her argument is more subtle than that of Menenius, who simply appeals for Coriolanus to make a rational compromise. Volumnia suggests that what he has to do is so remote from his true self that he can do it lightly, preserving his integrity beneath it. Cf. also Iago in *Othello*, who preserves his integrity by making this kind of *total* split between private and public personae; Iago preserves his identity by being the exact opposite of what he appears: 'I am not what I am' (I, 1). His tactics are not a diffusion of identity, like Lucio's in *Measure for Measure*, but a way of keeping himself intact.

He that trusts to you,
Where he should find you lions, finds you hares;*
Where foxes, geese; you are no surer, no,
Than is the coal of fire upon the ice
Or hailstone in the sun.   (I, 1)

It is the people's continual shifting of allegiance which he objects to; he dismisses them finally as 'fragments', men without integrity, lacking wholeness. He himself is 'constant', 'absolute'; he is unable to settle for half. He is, as Volumnia says,

Like to a harvest-man that's task'd to mow
Or all or lose his hire.   (I, 3)

When the messenger comes to Cominius with news of Coriolanus's army, he explains that his message is delayed because the enemy forced him to 'wheel three or four miles about'. The point is not laboured, but this is the kind of reasoned tactic which contrasts with Coriolanus's fanatical singlemindedness – he would have cut through the enemy, not avoided them.

But Coriolanus's enemies, and especially Brutus and Sicinius, show up the opposite danger, that of sheer opportunism, a tactical sense which is shifty rather than prudent. Brutus and Sicinius begin with a real desire to safeguard the people against tyranny, and this in some sense continues through all their manoeuvring; but to achieve this desire they are forced into an expediency which destroys what integrity they might have had. They come to work on a purely existential reaction to

---

* This same image is used by Cressida in *Troilus* to suggest, as here, inauthenticity, complete dislocation of self and action: 'They that have the voice of lions and the act of hares, are they not monsters?' (III, 2)

circumstances, seizing an opportunity where they can, without any consistent principle: the genuine purposes they began with are strangled in the detail of their working-out.

Coriolanus, against this, has a spontaneity which could be valuable, but it is the spontaneity of fire, uncontrollable, consuming, and disproportionate to its cause: he is, as Menenius says about himself, 'hasty and tinder-like upon too trivial motion', and a spark is enough to set him raging. The disproportionate quality of his action is emphasised by a persistent sense of superfluity: action which creates its own purposes and justification will naturally be freed from conventional limits and proportions. In the first scene of the play the first citizen mentions that Coriolanus has faults 'with surplus'; and it is surplus, imbalance, which character-ises his action throughout the play, in his individual stance against a city, his readiness to 'gird the gods' when moved to action, his personal banishing of Rome. The quality of disproportion goes with that of self-destruction, as Cominius sees:

> That is the way to lay the city flat,
> To bring the roof to the foundation,
> And bury all which yet distinctly ranges
> In heaps and piles of ruin.   (III, 1)

Civil conflict in Rome will bring down the roofs; Brutus and Sicinius have helped to 'melt the city leads upon (their) pates'. It is for a disproportionate sense of value that Coriolanus is finally condemned by Aufidius:

> At a few drops of women's rheum, which are
> As cheap as lies, he sold the blood and labour
> Or our great action . . .   (V, 6)

By being true to himself, Coriolanus is false to others, by being spontaneous he is irresponsible. He can only be himself: but to remain committed to himself in the face of social demands on him is to be disruptive. His inability to compromise is simultaneously a sign of personal wholeness and a cause of social disaster. The other patricians see that some kind of fusion of responsibility and authenticity is needed: Volumnia says her son is 'too absolute':

> Honour and policy, like unsever'd friends,
> I' th' war do grow together; grant that, and tell me
> In peace what each of them by th' other lose
> That they combine not there.   (III, 2)

But in practice, Volumnia's synthesis seem impossible to achieve. Cominius is perhaps the only character who actively lives a fusion of this kind, as we see when he addresses his soldiers on the battlefield:

> Breathe you, my friends. Well fought; we are come off
> Like Romans, neither foolish in our stands
> Nor cowardly in retire. Believe me, sirs,
> We shall be charg'd again. Whiles we have struck,
> By interims and conveying gusts we have heard
> The charges of our friends. The Roman gods,
> Lead their successes as we wish our own,
> That both our powers, with smiling fronts encount'ring,
> May give you thankful sacrifice!   (I, 6)

Cominius's willingness to let his troops rest contrasts with Coriolanus's ruthless demand for continual action: for Coriolanus, action generates its own value, for Cominius action is rationally directed towards an end. Cominius praises his men's performance and yet acknowledges the claims of prudence: they have been

neither foolhardy nor over-cautious. The immediacy
of the fighting has not prevented him from keeping a
general design in view, and planning ahead: they will
be charged again, and must be ready. Moreover,
engagement in their own activity has not excluded a
continual awareness of their fellow-soldiers: they have
listened in the process of fighting to the sounds of the
battle elsewhere. This is the kind of fusion which Coriolanus lacks: simultaneous self-awareness and awareness
of others. Cominius wishes the other soldiers the same
luck as his own men and himself: there is a sense of
shared life, of reciprocity, with the others, and their
eventual meeting will be on both sides an 'encounter',
of equals and friends. This will not be, however, an
enclosed encounter, as Coriolanus's encounters with
Aufidius are enclosed, shutting out the world: the two
sides will meet each other face to face but will be united
at the same time under the gods, to whom they will
jointly give sacrifice: their encounter will be both reciprocal and directed outwards, beyond themselves. The
same sense of unity and shared life with others emerges
in Cominius's command, later, to Titus Lartius:

> You, Titus Lartius,
> Must to Corioli back. Send us to Rome
> The best, with whom we may articulate
> For their own good and ours.   (I, 9)

This is the unity, the reciprocity with others, which
Coriolanus lacks: he is a public figure who is, ironically,
a completely private man. His tragedy lies in this division; it lies, too, in the intensity with which he stays
committed to himself in spite of all the wrongness of
this commitment. He stays committed because it is his

nature to be always wholly himself, even when he is pushed beyond the borders of society, betrayed and murdered. The tragic value lies ultimately in this wholeness, even though the wholeness was in part illusory, attained only by exclusion and blindness; it lies in the intensity of energy with which a human position is held and maintained, even though the position is intolerable. It is this paradox which takes us on to *Antony and Cleopatra*.

*   *   *

The starting-point for discussion of *Antony and Cleopatra* can be the same as for *Coriolanus*, the reply of the first citizen in the opening scene of that play to Menenius's question 'Will you undo yourselves?'—'We cannot, sir; we are undone already'. Antony and Cleopatra live throughout the whole play at this point: they are undone, they have touched the lowest point of abasement and dissolution, and are therefore in a position of desperate strength, capable of joy. To live out any kind of experience intensely, to the end, is to reach a growing-point of value, even, ironically, if the experience itself is sheerly negative; it is through an intensity of commitment that value can be created. To believe this is to believe that all experiences are equal, that value is cancelled; if all experiences, intensely explored, can yield value, then everything is equally valuable, and choice becomes gratuitous. But the sense that all experiences are equally valuable lies close to the sense that they are all equally valueless: intrinsic values are cancelled so that personal creation of value is possible, but the cancellation can breed a sense of emptiness which interacts

with the personal creation of meaning, giving it a desperate, neurotic quality. Again, tragic loss lies very
close to triumph, absurdity to an acceptance of all
things: if intrinsic meanings no longer exist, all experience can be felt as either equally acceptable or
equally absurd. This feeling can be traced particularly
in an attitude to action: if actions are valueless in themselves, then action or inaction become valuable only by
being consciously chosen, chosen with an awareness of
the gratuitousness of any choice which intensifies the
sense of personal creativity in choosing and acting.
But the sense of gratuitousness, of absurdity, may break
through the conscious choice and become dominant,
spoiling the action; the sense of personal creative power
and control may turn into a sense of futility. To be at
the peak of personal creation, forging private value and
a private reality, is to be also at the peak of an awareness
of chaos, of the inevitable arbitrariness of what is
created. It is only by holding to the personal creation
with a deep intensity of energy that it can be pushed
through into permanent value, finally clear of tragedy;
but the final securing of value in this way will always
involve death.

Antony and Cleopatra is about this kind of paradox,
as it affects a whole relationship, and the play itself is
at the point where its two central characters move, the
point of balance between utter desperation and utter
triumph. It is a commonplace that the line between
comedy and tragedy in the play is very thin, but the
significance of this to the play's themes has not always
been noticed. Some of the tragic or potentially tragic
scenes in the play are very near to comedy: Cleopatra's
beating of the servant who brings her news of Antony's

marriage to Octavia, and the whole of the death-scene of Antony, with its comic devices of mistake and irony, are two obvious instances. If the tragic feeling were slightly more intense it could become high comedy: in this way Shakespeare uses a familiar dramatic feeling to focus, in the actual structure of the play, the paradoxical closeness of creation and destruction which forms a major theme within it.

The idea of self-defeating action, as in *Coriolanus*, is dominant in the play: action is continually seen as involving its own breakdown, processes are constantly changing into their opposites. When the Egyptian fleet loses to Octavius, Antony has a sharp sense of absurdity:

> Now all labour
> Mars what it does; yea, very force entangles
> Itself with strength.   (IV, 14) .

He is prepared to take (and finally does take) the ultimate self-defeating action possible to a man, suicide. The condition of civil war which calls him back to Italy is one of a gratuitous expenditure of energies:

> . . . quietness, grown sick of rest, would purge
> By any desperate change.   (I, 3)

Cleopatra says Antony's vows 'break themselves in swearing'; Caesar warns Antony not to allow Octavia, the bond of their unity, to become the ram to batter it down; Pompey tells Menecrates that while they are suitors, 'decays the thing we sue for'; Octavia complains when her husband and brother are in conflict that her prayer will be self-defeating whatever side she prays for; Enobarbus sees irrational valour as eating the sword it fights with. The idea of self-consuming action is epitomised in Caesar's description of the people as a tide which goes backwards and forwards, 'to rot itself with motion'.

Antony's action is self-defeating in two ways. His action in relationship with Cleopatra is self-consuming, part of an inbound exchange of energies: the couple are caught up in an enclosed reciprocity which excludes the world except as it can be translated into their own private terms. His public action is self-defeating because it is done gratuitously, without a real sense of value or purpose. His attitude to public action is expressed in his approach to the battle with Octavius: he decides to fight by sea, against all rational advice, and having taken the decision stands by it:

> ANTONY Canidius, we
>   Will fight with him by sea.
>
> CLEOPATRA By sea! What else?
>
> CANIDIUS Why will my lord do so?
>
> ANTONY For that he dares us to't. (III, 7)

It is because action is meaningless to Antony unless it can be seen within the terms of his relationship with Cleopatra and therefore transformed into value that he is prepared to act quite gratuitously. Action is meaningless in itself, as it was meaningful in itself to Coriolanus: in both cases inherent, rational value is ignored in favour of a merely private creation of meaning.

Antony, like Coriolanus, is confronted with a choice between personal self-fulfilment and social responsibility, and he choose self-fulfilment; but unlike Corio-

lanus, he approaches the choice with full, tragic consciousness of his condition, and chooses with an element
of gratuitousness. Coriolanus, in placing his personal
authenticity above responsibility to others, could hardly
help himself: his inability to be other than himself is
at the root of his tragedy. But with Antony, the pressures in both directions are powerful and felt: we see
him pulled both ways during the play. Any final
commitment made in this situation must therefore have
a tragic quality, precisely because it is a commitment
taken deliberately, with an awareness of other possibilities. Antony chooses Egypt and lives his choice with the
conscious intensity of a man aware that he is creating,
through the sheer force of his energy, a whole life out
of what is inevitably partial. 'There's not a minute of
our lives should stretch/Without some pleasure now',
he tells Cleopatra, and the calculated recklessness of
this is significant of his position. Antony's attitude
throughout approaches his final attitude to death:

> But I will be
> A bridegroom in my death, and run into't
> As to a lover's bed.   (IV, 14)

He creates value consciously out of chaos, embracing it
and therefore making it significant and fruitful, as
the action of the sun quickens the Nile's slime into
fertile life.

From Octavius's viewpoint it is waste, superfluity,
which is Antony's vice: he is self-squandering, burning
up energies which could be socially useful and are
urgently needed in Rome. But to Antony it is the very
superabundance of the energy which he expends in his
relationship with Cleopatra which is the basis of value:

value grows within intensity and excess, defeating the
objective, balanced proportions of Rome, the measure
and reckoning which Antony scorns in his first words in
the play. The rejection of conventional proportions, the
celebration of excess, is both destructive waste and creative superabundance: Antony moves at the point of
fusion of the two, the point where each blends into the
other. Antony and Cleopatra's rejection of Roman
measurements is part of the whole texture of their
relationship, not only in their self-squandering, but in
the disproportion of perspective, the close, vivid intensity with which odd details are focused in their
minds, the remembering of scraps of past experience
and precious moments. The rejection of a received
scale of values is closely connected, as in previous plays,
with a rejection of the whole machinery of rational
thinking and comparison. Antony's description of a
crocodile to Lepidus typifies this:

> It is shap'd, sir, like itself, and it is as broad as it hath breadth;
> it is just so high as it is, and moves with it own organs. It lives
> by that which nourisheth it, and the elements once out of it, it
> transmigrates.   (II, 7)

Antony succeeds in saying nothing about the crocodile
except that it is what it is: when objective meanings and
values are cancelled, things are merely individual,
uniquely themselves, defying comparison as Antony's
own relationship with Cleopatra defies comparison.
Cleopatra, too, is a 'lass unparalleled', who 'beggars all
description'.

In *Coriolanus*, Menenius and Volumnia worked for
a compromise between authenticity and responsibility;
in this play, Lepidus is the compromise-figure, offering

a prudent solution to Antony and Octavius, trying to patch together quarrels and temper extremes. But Lepidus is a living image of the impoverishment of this politic moderation, a man without integrity: he flatters and is flattered by Antony and Octavius, but engages the genuine care and attention of neither of them. Cleopatra bitingly satirises the judicious mean he stands for, in a different context, when she rails against Antony:

CLEOPATRA What, was he sad or merry?

ALEXAS Like to the time o' th' year between the extremes
Of hot and cold; he was nor sad nor merry.

CLEOPATRA O well-divided disposition! Note him,
Note him, good Charmian; 'tis the man; but note him!
He was not sad, for he would shine on those
That make their looks by his; he was not merry,
Which seem'd to tell them his remembrance lay
In Egypt with his joy; but between both.
O heavenly mingle!   (I, 5)

This kind of prudent avoidance of extremes is seen as inauthentic, not helpful: it is a liberal compromise which solves nothing and merely dilutes the seriousness and strength of the problems at the heart of the play. To make a commitment may be disastrous, but to avoid one is to surrender integrity, to lose that wholeness which comes only from full engagement. When life is forced to an extreme, no compromise is possible, and a tragic choice must be made: Octavia discovers this, when her loyalty is torn between Antony and Octavius:

Husband win, win brother,
Prays, and destroys the prayer; no mid-way
'Twixt these extremes at all.   (III, 4)

However authenticity and responsibility are to be reconciled, it will not be by gently toning down either or both: Antony and Cleopatra reject this kind of half-measure, and by remaining intensely committed to each other they achieve a wholeness which would not otherwise be available. This personal creation remains valuable, as the product of human energy and involvement, despite the fact that the energies are anti-social, the involvement a private one in the margins of the common life. Cleopatra is Shakespeare's most complete image of fully authentic life: she cancels and re-creates all values in herself, so that all creation becomes valuable by being part of her:

> Age cannot wither her, nor custom stale
> Her infinite variety. Other women cloy
> The appetites they feed, but she makes hungry
> Where most she satisfies; for vilest things
> Become themselves in her, that the holy priests
> Bless her when she is riggish.   (II, 2)

Everything becomes her: 'to chide, to laugh, to weep'; every passion strives to make itself 'fair and admir'd' in her. She reconciles and renews all things within a continual, self-refreshing spontaneity, making them holy because authentically *her*.

Antony and Cleopatra explores one response to the problem of reconciling authentic and responsible living, a response in which one aspect of the dilemma is taken, chosen, and lived to the full with tragic affirmation. The result is a new insight into the depth of authentic life which will have to be part of any attempt to make this life responsible, to put it back within society.

CHAPTER FIVE

Macbeth

Macbeth centres around a single action – the murder of Duncan – which, like the action of Coriolanus and Antony, is seen as self-defeating. The whole structure of the play makes this clear: Scotland moves from health to sickness and back into health, Malcolm replaces Duncan, and the wheel comes full circle without Macbeth having made any permanent achievement. The energy he expends in trying to secure his position contrasts ironically with this lack of attainment: his actions are cancelled out by the circular movement of the play, and he becomes a momentary aberration in Scotland's history, an aberration without lasting consequence: the history rights itself and continues. Macbeth's action in killing Duncan is marred by a literal sterility: he will have no sons to make his achievement permanently fruitful. But the action is inherently sterile, too, and it is this paradox which the play builds on: an action intended as creative, self-definitive, is in fact destructive, self-undoing.

Macbeth becomes king of Scotland between the end of Act II and the beginning of Act III, but in achieving the status which he saw previously as ultimate, he finds that his troubles have in fact only just begun: he spends the rest of the play fighting to secure his role. He fights to *become* what, objectively, he is: to clear up and tidy the straggling consequences of his action and settle down in the achieved and perfected definition of kingship:

> To be thus is nothing,
> But to be safely thus.   (III, 1)

The idea of a perfected, completely achieved act is insistent in the play: Macbeth upbraids the witches as 'imperfect speakers', and his reaction to the news of Fleance's escape focusses his frustration as continually falling short of full achievement:

> I had else been perfect,
> Whole as the marble, founded as the rock,
> As broad and general as the casing air,
> But now I am cabin'd, cribb'd, confin'd, bound in
> To saucy doubts and fears.   (III, 3)

Every action done to attain security mars itself: every act has a built-in flaw, a consequence which escapes, like Fleance, from the control of the actor and returns to plague him. Macbeth cannot achieve a pure act, a wholeness: his actions unravel themselves, and he longs for a pure act as he longs for the sleep which 'knits up the ravell'd sleave of care':

> If it were done, when 'tis done, then 'twere well
> It were done quickly. If th'assassination
> Could trammel up the consequence, and catch,
> With his surcease, success; that but this blow
> Might be the be-all and the end-all here—
> But here upon this bank and shoal of time—
> We'd jump the life to come. But in these cases
> We still have judgment here, that we but teach
> Bloody instructions, which being taught return
> To plague th'inventor.   (I, 7)

Macbeth wants the action without the consequences, without the uncontrollable, multiplying effects; he dreams of an action which contains and controls all its results within itself. He also wants achievement without the process of reaching it, as Lady Macbeth sees:

> Thou wouldst be great;
> Art not without ambition, but without
> The illness should attend it. What thou wouldst highly,
> That wouldst thou holily; wouldst not play false,
> And yet wouldst wrongly win.   (I, 4)

But the irony implicit in all action is precisely that any achievement involves a process of reaching and a process of results, and both processes can destroy what is attained. Macbeth wants the static, permanent status of kingship without the fluid, temporal process of actions necessary to win and secure it; he finds that kingship is for him only a process, not the complete definition it was for Duncan. Having become king officially by killing Duncan, he finds that he has achieved nothing: there is always another step to be taken before he is *really* king, secure in his role, and each step taken undoes what he has won because each step breeds more destructive consequences. He is not allowed to become what he is, to be, authentically, king; he spends all his time and energy in consolidating his position and is therefore unable to enjoy kingship at all. He is a man pursuing his own act, chasing himself; his action in killing Duncan both makes and mars him, as drink, according to the Porter, makes and mars a man.

Macbeth's condition is imaged especially in the recurrent metaphor of ill-fitting robes. When Ross and

Angus greet him with the title of Cawdor he asks why they dress him in borrowed robes, and Banquo's aside when Macbeth is 'rapt' after the witches' promise captures the significance of this:

> New honours come upon him,
> Like our strange garments, cleave not to their mould
> But with the aid of use.   (I, 3)

A role or title can be laid externally on a man, but he must then make it his own, moulding it like new clothes to his own shape so that it is authentic, not external any longer. It is not enough to be Cawdor or king in a merely objective way, as in *Measure for Measure* it is not enough to conform externally to the law; Macbeth sees that he must become, genuinely, what he is officially, authenticate his new name so that he can live it by habit, as in the Last Comedies virtue is a habitual living of the law.* The importance of names and titles is stressed in the play: Macbeth is given, ceremonially, the former title of Cawdor; Macduff, discovering the murder of Duncan, says it is a deed which tongue and heart 'cannot conceive nor name'; the witches perform 'a deed without a name'; Macbeth is a 'tyrant, whose sole name blisters our tongues', as Malcolm says. In all these cases, names have a peculiarly creative power:

---

* Note also that Lady Macbeth prays for the strength, not simply to *do* evil, but to *become* evil, authentically, to be transformed into a woman whose desires as well as actions are unnatural:

> Come, you spirits
> That tend on mortal thoughts, unsex me here;
> And fill me, from the crown to the toe, top-full
> Of direst cruelty.   (I, 5)

'Fullness' expresses this authentic life, as it does with Duncan, whose 'plenteous joys' are 'wanton in fullness'.   (I, 4) things without names are beyond the reach of human meanings, part of the nothingness of the evil lying at the edges of the human community. To receive a name is to be something positive, to have a sanctioned place within the community.

Macbeth's murder of Duncan is a falling from such a place within the community to the pure negativity of evil, the area of nameless deeds. Before the murder, Macbeth's authentic life consists in serving Duncan, and the service is not an external, mechanical obedience but a living self-expression: he wants no reward for his allegiance because

> The service and the loyalty I owe,
> In doing it, pays itself.   (I, 4)

He needs no external payment, but is paid by the deed itself; the circularity here is that of the fusion of authentic and responsible action, not the self-destroying circularity which is Macbeth's later condition. It is in Duncan's service that Macbeth finds personal joy: 'The rest is labour, which is not us'd for you' (I, 4). In destroying Duncan, Macbeth is destroying himself: his own life and peace is in Duncan's possession, and the murder is thus an act of self-violence. It is a self-destroying act, one done to achieve a happiness lost in the very moment of trying to attain it; his action, like his ambition, 'o'er-leaps itself, And falls on the other' (I, 7). In destroying Duncan he is being inauthentic, less than himself: he overreaches himself, falling away from his own positive life into negativity:

> I dare do all that may become a man;
> Who dares do more is none.   (I, 7)

To overreach one's limits is to be less than oneself, to undo oneself; authentic living consists in staying freely within these limits of nature, recognising them as creative. To try to be more than human is to be an animal: evil is a kind of failure, a meaninglessness. This is what Lady Macbeth cannot see: to her a man can create his own limits, pushing them out to suit his ambition:

> When you durst do it, then you were a man;
> And to be more than what you were, you would
> Be so much more the man.   (I, 7)

Macbeth takes her advice and goes beyond the limits of humanity in an attempt to be more fully human; in trying to achieve a title he goes beyond all names, all definitions, into the negation of evil and chaos. Lady Macbeth cannot see that limits are not what restrict humanity but what make it what it is, as a name creates in defining, in limiting.

Lady Macbeth's attitude to her husband's action is very close to the kind of gratuitous commitment which we have seen in the Roman Plays. She accuses Macbeth of forcing a dislocation in himself between impulse and action: she sees him as inauthentic, less than a full man, because he is afraid of spontaneously enacting his desires. In taking this stance she ignores all considerations of responsibility in action: to be a true man is to act on one's desires, regardless of the harm this may cause. If a man takes a decision he must hold to it, quite gratuitously, in spite of other claims:

> I have given suck, and know
> How tender 'tis to love the babe that milks me—
> I would, while it was smiling in my face,

> Have pluck'd my nipple from his boneless gums,
> And dash'd the brains out, had I so sworn
> As you have done to this.   (I, 7)

The gratuitousness of Lady Macbeth's commitment becomes, finally, the desperate and lavish gratuitousness of Macbeth in the last scenes of the play, when all hope of re-integrating with his society has gone. Macbeth fights in the play to consolidate the position he has snatched, to make it fully his, but each step he takes – the murder of Banquo, the slaughter of Macduff's wife and children – undoes him further, in a continuously self-defeating process. He is unable to rest in achievement: this is why he envies the perfected quiet of Duncan in his grave, who has reached the ultimately static condition of death:

> 'Tis safer to be that which we destroy,
> Than by destruction dwell in doubtful joy.   (III, 2)

The tension breaks at last, and he becomes fully conscious of the absurdity of his own self-defeating activity:

> I am in blood
> Stepp'd in so far that, should I wade no more,
> Returning were as tedious as go o'er.   (III, 4)

The point of gratuitousness is reached here, as it was in *Antony and Cleopatra*. Macbeth has undone himself so far that he may as well go on: he has touched rock-bottom, and his future action will now be inevitably creative, since he can destroy himself no more. The creativity may be merely a gratuitous self-expenditure, a desperate celebration of action-for-action's-sake, of the absurd; to know he cannot win brings a new kind of strength, as a complete lack of value gives the first murderer a reckless power. The murderer is a man

> ... So weary with disasters, tugg'd with fortune,
> That I would set my life on any chance,
> To mend it or be rid on't.   (III, 1)

Lady Macbeth's remedy is an equally desperate stoicism:

> Things without all remedy
> Should be without regard. What's done is done.   (III, 2)

and Ross's comment on the condition of Scotland expresses the same feeling:

> Things at the worst will cease, or else climb upward
> To what they were before.   (IV, 2)

Macbeth's attempts to create meaning from a world which Duncan's death drained of value degenerate finally into the peace of embracing chaos, accepting meaninglessness: life is a succession of tomorrows, a tale told by an idiot, and having recognised this he can fight till the flesh is hacked from his bones, trying to the last. He will at least die in harness, enjoying action for its own sake, spending himself freely in his final moments. He can find comfort in absurdity, as he finds constancy in inconstancy:

> Come what come may,
> Time and the hour runs through the roughest day.   (I, 3)

There is no final answer in this for Shakespeare, any more than there is in *Antony and Cleopatra*; Macbeth, like Antony, undoes himself in rejecting social responsibility, and whatever value can be forcibly created from the rejection must be inevitably marginal. The main exploration must still be towards a way of discovering a mode of social responsibility which can fully contain and express individual drives of the power and depth of those we see at work in *Macbeth*, and this will mean moving beyond a kind of energy which is formidable in its human strength, but negative at root.

CHAPTER SIX

The Winter's Tale and The Tempest

THE breakdown which we have explored in the problem plays and tragedies between spontaneity and reason, authenticity and responsibility, can be seen, generally, as a breakdown between individual and society. This is in itself too simple a formula to be really helpful: it can provide a framework, but not a substitute, for analysis of what is actually wrong in the texture of a society's experience. But there are points where it is helpful to reduce the complex analysis to this basic term, and to come to the Last Comedies from the problem plays and tragedies seems to be such a point. The Last Comedies reveal an exploration of familiar themes in the context of a wholly different conception of the relation of individual and society; this is not a matter of intellectual adjustment, but a different texture of feeling in the plays, a new way of looking at character and environment.

In the first scene of The Winter's Tale, the young prince Mamillius is described by Camillo in almost religious terms:

> It is a gallant child; one that indeed physics the subject, makes old hearts fresh; they that went on crutches ere he was born desire yet their life to see him a man. (I, 1)

Mamillius is the focus of the creative life of the court, the centre of loving attention: the court Ladies hang on his every word, flirting with him like a lover. For Leontes, he is a living image of his own life, almost as close to him as he is to himself: they are 'almost as like as eggs'. When Hermione is cut off from Mamillius, she is ready to die. Similarly, Mamillius's personal life is nourished by the court's life, as it is focused, especially, in the love-relationship of his parents; when this life is destroyed by Leontes's jealousy, he pines away and dies. His death strikes in turn at the root of the society he lives in, causing its final disintegration in the 'death' of Hermione, the breaking of Leontes, the loss of Perdita, Camillo and Antigonus. The removal of Mamillius drains the creative life of the court: the community of love which he bound together falls apart as he dies.

This sense of a deep connectedness of lives is at the root of the Last Comedies. Personal life is not independent of the community; it is derived from it, and survives only in terms of it. Similarly, the community survives only in terms of the personal lives which create and sustain it: the life of a whole society is dependent for its quality on the life of particular individuals within it, individuals who focus and embody common feelings. In one sense, of course, this is not a new development in Shakespeare: most of the major tragedies reveal a crucial interdependence between the personal action of individuals and the life of a whole society. But this connection is less deep and less integral than in the Last Comedies: Macbeth's personal actions have deep effects on his society, but we can still feel Macbeth and his society as separate terms, although closely related. The personal lives of Leontes, Prospero, Miranda, Mamillius, however, are fused with the life

of their community at so deep a level that action which is
wholly personal, love and anger and fidelity, is simultaneously social; the relation between social and personal
in these plays is not just one of physical consequence
or circumstance, but the relation of aspects of a single
life. A society is available to us in the plays as a web of
relationships which are personal, and yet point beyond
themselves to a shared life not reducible to individual
components.

The Winter's Tale, therefore, does not show a society
disintegrate as the *consequence* of personal behaviour,
and re-knit as the consequence of the behaviour of
others. This is an acceptable reading at one level, but
it misses the fact that the relation of personal behaviour
to society is not experienced in the play as one of practical consequences but as a simultaneity, a fusion of two
kinds of life which grow from the same root. The court
society of Sicilia does not disintegrate as a *result* of
Leontes's evil and Mamillius's death: it is *in* the breakdown of the individual life, the personal relationship,
that the whole fabric of a community falls apart. The
feeling here is close to that of *Troilus and Cressida*,
where in a similar way one kind of life could exist in
terms of another: Troy stands, as Nestor says, 'in' the
weakness of the Greeks and not in her own strength,
taking personal life wholly from the context of the
Greeks' failure. Again, it is 'in' Achilles, Hector, Helen
Ajax, that the fortunes of each side are at various points
focused and contained, so that a personal failing will be
simultaneously a social disaster. In the Last Comedies,
individual lives are rooted into a community, and to
effect or damage one part of the delicate network of
relationships is to affect or damage the whole. Polixenes

realises this when he demands to be informed of the
changed situation in the court after Leontes's outburst
of jealousy:

> Good Camillo,
> Your chang'd complexions are to me a mirror
> Which shows me mine chang'd too; for I must be
> A party in this alteration, finding
> Myself thus alter'd with't.   (I, 2)

The individual life is caught up in any general alteration of feeling: Polixenes finds his personal fortunes
reflected in the community which moulds them, in the
faces of others; he can only know his own situation in
terms of the general conditions from which it derives.
Individual actions have multiple effects: Leontes's
madness kills Mamillius and loses him Hermione,
Perdita, Camillo, Antigonus and Polixenes; the union
of Perdita and Florizel effects the union of Leontes and
Hermione, Leontes and Polixenes, Polixenes and
Florizel, Perdita and Leontes, Paulina and Antigonus.
The fusion of personal and social is reflected in the
idea of a personal action which is also public, modifying
a whole society; in *The Tempest*, as we shall see later,
the play itself can be understood as both a record of
complex public events and a single, personal act of
Prospero's.

The simultaneity of social and personal life is there,
in *The Winter's Tale*, in the fact that the relationship
between Sicilia and Bohemia is both personal and political, each in terms of the other. Leontes and Polixenes
have been forced to part since their boyhood, but their
personal relationship has continued and found mature
expression in political union:

Since their more mature dignities and royal necessities made separation of their society, their encounters, though not personal, have been royally attorneyed with interchange of gifts, letters, loving embassies; that they have seemed to be together, though absent; shook hands, as over a vast; and embrac'd as it were from the ends of opposed winds.   (I, 1)

Camillo says these encounters are not 'personal', but this is true only in a limited sense of the term; it is part of maturity to be able to see 'personal' relationship as extending beyond obvious physical presence, and harmonising with public function. Leontes and Polixenes have grown out of the immediately personal, physical relationship of boyhood, the state in which they were as 'twinn'd lambs' who knew no evil, into a personal relationship which exists in terms of their formal roles in society; there is a complete fusion between their social and personal selves, and this is a measure of their maturity. Personal relationship no longer exists outside society, beyond responsibility, but is now expressed in terms of a whole community and its formal institutions. When the personal relationship breaks down, so does the political: not as a consequence, but because each exists in terms of the other.

The same simultaneity of the deeply personal and the formally social, of private and public, is expressed intricately in the tone and form of the conversation between Leontes, Hermione and Polixenes in Act I Scene 2, where Leontes and Hermione are trying to persuade Polixenes to extend his stay in Sicilia. The quality of personal desire for Polixenes's presence, and the deeply formal quality of expression and persuasion, are precisely balanced: the conversation is conducted like a piece of diplomatic manœuvring, but the manœuvring and argument grow directly out of the personal love between Leontes, Hermione, and Polixenes. Polixenes declares that he must leave Sicilia, and states the exact length of time he has been absent from home: 'nine changes of the wat'ry star' have gone by, and his social duties press him to return. Leontes makes an appeal himself, and then requests Hermione to speak; Hermione speaks first through Leontes, and then directly to Polixenes. The formal quality of this is intensified by the terms on which Hermione appeals: she makes her request depend, not on depth of personal feeling, but on personal feeling expressed in terms of exact reckoning:

> . . . Yet of your royal presence I'll adventure
> The borrow of a week. When at Bohemia
> You take my lord, I'll give him my commission
> To let him there a month behind the gest
> Prefix'd for's parting.—Yet, good deed, Leontes,
> I love thee not a jar o' th' clock behind
> What lady she her lord.   (I, 2)

Hermione is making a formal bargain with Polixenes, exchanging an extended stay for him in Sicilia for a longer stay for Leontes when he visits Bohemia; her final statement that she loves Leontes just as much as any other woman loves her husband (measured to the actual tick of a clock) images this fusion of personal feeling and formal precision. Love is contained and expressed within public form, moving freely within defining limits, as the personal love of Leontes and Polixenes is contained within their public relationship. Public, precise form does not restrict personal feeling but brings it to a fully mature, responsible expression, so that spontaneous love and social duty are united, private and public fused.

It is because Leontes thinks that his wife has overstepped the precise limits of friendship with Polixenes that he is maddened with jealousy. Hermione's love for Polixenes is real and free, not merely dutiful but authentic; but it must find expression within the socially verified limits of their relationship as friend and friend's wife, or it becomes something different, adultery. Hermione herself finds no tension in this: her personal and social selves are in exact fusion:

> . . . For Polixenes,
> With whom I am accus'd, I do confess
> I lov'd him as in honour he requir'd;
> With such a kind of love as might become
> A lady like me; with a love even such,
> So and no other, as yourself commanded . . .   (III, 2)

She has not gone 'one jot beyond the bond of honour' either in act or will; her love is free and generous, but instinctively confined to what is proper to being a Queen. There is no need for Leontes to imprison Hermione in case she acts treacherously; her life, her thoughts and desires, are spontaneously confined to what is proper, naturally and habitually good. In traditional terms, she is virtuous, she has the habit of goodness. Hermione is a living fusion of spontaneous and responsible life: it is part of her authentic nature to act well, and her love for Polixenes is neither constricted by public form nor artificially worked up, but most real when it is most properly confined.

Hermione's authenticity is expressed in the likeness

of both Mamillius and Perdita to their father. Mamillius
is an exact copy of Leontes, and so is Perdita:

> Behold, my lords,
> Although the print be little, the whole matter
> And copy of the father—eye, nose, lip,
> The trick of 's frown, his forehead . . .
> The very mould and frame of hand, nail, finger.   (II, 3)

Hermione's truth and integrity is manifested in the
exactness of relation between her husband and her
children, between the personal life she shares with
Leontes and its fruit, its actions. The 'mould' of the
child fully contains and expresses the wedded life of
Leontes and Hermione, as Julietta's womb in *Measure
for Measure* contained and fully expressed the life of
Claudio. There is no breakdown, no dislocation between
this personal life and its social, tangible results in Mamillius and Perdita; Hermione's children are in spontaneous continuity with her husband, authentic and
exact expressions of the couple's mutual life. Leontes
fails to see this in the case of Perdita: he accuses Hermione of falseness because he sees her as publicly
claiming as their mutually self-expressive act a child
which he believes to be the result of her private, ille-
gitimate encounter with Polixenes. In disowning Perdita he is disowning his own act, denying himself.
Hermione, in contrast, remains committed to her act,
totally authentic: she is as she appears, and the likeness
of her children to her husband is, as Paulina sees, a
living image of this continuity of self.

The accusation of Hermione is seen by the court as
an accusation of all women: if Hermione is really false,
then every inch and dram of women's flesh in the world

is false. Hermione focuses a whole community, indeed a whole race: what happens to her in personal terms happens simultaneously to a whole society. But she is not merely a cypher: she is a real woman, in real relationships. The fusion of personal and social, of individual and society, does not mean that the individual is reduced to a purely symbolic function; on the contrary, it is in the very reality and intensity of the individual and the personal relationship that a society can be destroyed or healed. In shattering real personal relationships, Leontes shatters a whole society, leaving it heirless and bereaved; in forming a truly personal love-relationship, Perdita and Florizel can restore the community to health.

It is important to see that this relationship of Perdita and Florizel is not instrumental only in the practical sense that it is by the union of the heirs of both kings that Sicilia and Bohemia can be re-united. The significance of the pastoral scene of Act IV Scene 4 is that the growth of creative life in the love of Perdita and Florizel, a growth nourished by a whole community, *coincides* with the slow growth of Leontes in Sicilia towards self-reconciliation and repentence. Again, it is in and through the relationship of Perdita and Florizel, and the creative life which it releases, that Leontes can be healed; his restoration is effected not merely by the physical gaining of an heir, but by the general movement of love which the particular relationship of Perdita and Florizel both focuses and creates. The movement, as with Mamillius, is reciprocal: individual human beings, particular relationships, embody and make active the creative life of a community, which in turn sustains and nourishes them. Mamillius, Hermione, Florizel and

Perdita are both creators and created; they draw life
from the richness of a community and return it in an
enriching movement, deepening the common life
which feeds them. Their personal life is threatened or
actually crushed by society, personified in Leontes, but
by crushing it the society does damage to itself, drains
itself of life.

This reciprocal movement is brought out in a different way in the play in the conversation between
Perdita and Polixenes about art and nature in the pastoral scene. Polixenes, defending the use of art to improve nature, points out that the art which is used is
itself created by nature:

> . . . nature is made better by no mean
> But nature makes that mean; so over that art,
> Which you say adds to nature, is an art
> That nature makes. You see, sweet maid, we marry
> A gentler scion to the wildest stock,
> And make conceive a bark of baser kind
> By bud of nobler race. This is an art
> Which does mend nature—change it rather; but
> The art itself is nature.   (IV, 4)

Nature creates the instrument of her own transfiguration: she is not merely a passive recipient of art, but
actively creates the art which changes her, in a mutually
interactive process. The relevance of this to the central
theme of the play is clear: Leontes, too, created the
instrument of his own transfiguration, so that as father,
and thus as actively creating, he must submit passively
to the transfiguring action of the daughter he has made.

The fusion of personal and social in the play is
closely related to this reciprocity. Individuals, as we
have seen, both draw life from a community and actively

shape it: they are active and passive simultaneously, subjectively shaping a society, as sources, and being shaped by it in return. But this is also the condition of a real equal relationship between two individuals: in a love-relationship both persons must give and receive simultaneously, each must be possessed and possessor in a mutual interaction. In this sense, the individual love-relationship can act as an ideal image of the reciprocal relation between man and society, and it is offered as this kind of image in *The Winter's Tale* and *The Tempest*. Moreover, the love-relationship involves a free and spontaneous self-giving within the defining limits of responsibility to another: love is the paradox of being simultaneously bound and free. In this way we can see how the themes we have explored converge in these plays into a unity, so that the synthesis of active and passive, subject and object, precision and freedom, social and personal, are aspects of the same synthesis.

The fullest reciprocity of selves, as we saw in *Measure for Measure*, is to be one flesh with another; it is therefore significant that in all the Last Comedies a physical family is at the centre.* Kinship is a major theme in the plays: the physical linking of human beings forms the basis for community, and for responsibility, as the Clown sees:

She being none of your flesh and blood, your flesh and blood has not offended the King; and so your flesh and blood is not to be punish'd by him. (IV, 4)

Mamillius, as we have seen already, is a copy of Leontes, a mirror of his life; he stands in the same relation to Leontes as Polixenes's son stands in to him:

* Antiochus and his daughter in *Pericles* are doubly two in one flesh, both as father and daughter and as man and wife.

He's all my exercise, my mirth, my matter;
Now my sworn friend, and then mine enemy;
My parasite, my soldier, statesman, all.   (I, 2)

The description is echoed in a different context later in
the Shepherd's rebuke to Perdita at the rustic festival:

Fie, daughter! When my old wife liv'd, upon
This day she was both pantler, butler, cook;
Both dame and servant; welcom'd all; serv'd all;
Would sing her song and dance her turn; now here
At upper end o' th' table, now i' th' middle . . .   (IV, 4)

To be all things to another, to share in all another's
experiences in a continual switching of roles and functions, is the fullest image of union with him: it is
equivalent to sharing his personal life, and demands the
kind of 'negative capability', the ability to dissolve into
events and others, epitomised in Ariel in *The Tempest*,
who is co-active with Prospero, cleaves to his thoughts.*
Mamillius, Hermione and Polixenes are all 'apparent
to (Leontes's) heart', and the image of closeness to the
heart, as in *Hamlet*, reflects a condition of intimate and
reciprocal union. Leontes has trusted Camillo 'with all
the nearest things to (his) heart', and it is this sense of
closeness to another, of shared identity, which motivates
the shock and rage at the idea of having been betrayed
by the other. To have been deceived by one apparent
to one's heart means to have been deceived in oneself;
Leontes, as Camillo sees, is 'in rebellion with himself':
his jealousy is a crisis of identity. To doubt the queen is

---

* The suggestion of Ariel in both these passages hints also at the closeness
of this kind of compassion to the dangerous diffusion or cancelling of
identity which Ariel, Hamlet and Osric show in different ways.

to doubt himself, and the whole of his previously securely-based reality, of which assurance of Hermione's virtue was an integral factor: if whispering and leaning cheek to cheek is nothing, then Bohemia and the world and everything is nothing. Leontes says this to show that the adultery is indeed real, since Bohemia is real, but what comes through powerfully, in opposition to his articulated meaning, is the agonised feeling that everything is nothing because Hermione is now nothing: reality itself is proved false. To have lost Hermione is to have lost himself and the world: Polixenes's innocent comment that the king looks as though he has lost a region 'lov'd as he loves himself' hits the truth exactly.

Self-knowledge, loving knowledge of another, and a role in the community are bound up together, as they were in *Measure for Measure*. Florizel's words to Perdita show this fusion of all three:

> . . . I cannot be
> Mine own, nor anything to any, if
> I be not thine.   (IV, 4)

Florizel will find himself, and therefore his true relation to a society, through his personal relationship with Perdita; in the same way, Perdita will find her true identity (quite literally), and therefore her place in society, through her love for Florizel. The self-exploration is reciprocal, done through one another, and yet it is directed outwards to society, not enclosed and circular. A true relationship is one in which a man can find simultaneously his authentic self and his relation to a society; in this sense, the love of Perdita and Florizel contrasts with the false relationship which Leontes

establishes between himself and Camillo in commanding
the latter to poison Polixenes:

> I must be the poisoner
> Of good Polixenes; and my ground to do't
> Is the obedience to a master; one
> Who, in rebellion with himself, will have
> All that are his so too.   (I, 2)

A man who is false to himself will be false to those who
derive their life from him: the alteration in the king
implies and effects an alteration in his servants. It is
because Leontes wears Camillo in his heart, and Camillo
lives only to be a faithful servant, that a self-divided
Leontes will mean a self-divided Camillo: they share a
single life, and distortion in one part of the fabric
creates distortion in the whole. Camillo's real self consists in serving Leontes: to be commanded by Leontes
to do evil therefore means that he must go counter to
his nature, his integrity, either in doing it or refusing
to do it: 'To do't, or no, is certain/To me a break-neck'.
He is faced with a choice between obedience and integrity, yet his integrity consists in his obedience: to be
untrue to Leontes is to be untrue to himself.

Camillo, then, is forced to choose between his authentic self and his obedience to Leontes, two aspects of
him which are generally one, and his relationship with
his master breaks down as a result. His relationship to
Leontes has not been equal, of course, but it has a
similar quality to the ideal relationship of Perdita and
Florizel. True relationship is to be *authentically* bound
by another, bound and responsible in a way which is
a full personal self-expression, which coincides with
one's personal desires. This is the condition which

Polixenes accepts when he consents to remain in Sicilia as Hermione's guest rather than as her prisoner: he is given a straight choice between being forced to stay, or making his own and accepting a bondage which is inevitable. Real relationship therefore involves being active and passive simultaneously: each person embraces and actively authenticates the bondage of the relationship, so that free and spontaneous love finds expression within a precise responsibility. Camillo's relationship with Polixenes, although again fundamentally unequal, is like this; Polixenes is anxious that Camillo should not leave him to return to Sicilia:

> As thou lov'st me, Camillo, wipe not out the rest of thy services by leaving me now. The need I have of thee thine own goodness hath made. Better not to have had thee than thus to want thee; thou, having made me businesses which none without thee can sufficiently manage, must either stay to execute them thyself, or take away with thee the very services thou hast done ... (IV, 2)

Camillo does not merely execute Polixenes's commands as an instrument, but is himself a source, actively organising and controlling affairs which none but he can manage, while being simultaneously bound in service to his master: he moves freely within precise limits.* It is Camillo's own goodness which has created the need Polixenes has of him, a need which inspires his services: the relationship, again, is one of mutual

---

* Contrast the Polixenes-Camillo relationship in this respect with Camillo's unashamed *use* of Autolycus: 'We'll make an instrument of this' (IV, 4); and compare their relationship to that of Ariel and Prospero in *The Tempest*, where Ariel is allowed similar range for personal inventiveness within a defined pattern of responsibility to his master.

dependence. Camillo is fully himself when he is fully serving others, as his words to Florizel suggests:

> It shall be so my care
> To have you royally appointed as if
> The scene you play were mine.   (IV, 3)

The case of Camillo points to the fundamentally conservative elements in Shakespeare's attitude in these plays: Shakespeare is concerned primarily, not that relationship should be equal, but that a relationship of service should be authenticated by the servant, made personal and living. The danger in this is obvious: Antonio in *The Tempest* made his tyrannical rule of Milan secure by setting 'all hearts i' th' state/To what tune pleas'd his ear', moulding the hearts, the authentic selves, of his subjects to his own designs. The process of authenticating the law can, if the law is tyrannical, be merely an authenticating of slavery, as we saw in *Hamlet*. The relationship of Polixenes and Camillo, like that of Prospero and Ariel in *The Tempest*, remains one of master-and-servant despite its reciprocity: the reciprocity merely confirms and reinforces the inequality. But the love-relationship of Florizel and Perdita is an instance of a mutuality which involves total equality: Polixenes's words to Perdita in the pastoral scene, after he has thrown off his disguise, emphasise unconsciously this mutuality:

> . . . if ever henceforth thou
> These rural latches to his entrance open,
> Or hoop his body more with thy embraces,
> I will devise a death as cruel for thee
> As thou art tender to't.   (IV, 4)

Polixenes's threat shows love both as a passive yielding ('These rural latches to his entrance open') and an active possession ('Or hoop his body more with thy embraces') in an almost single movement. The reciprocity is imaged again in the final two lines, where cruelty and tenderness, submission and forcing, stand in similar interrelation. It is Perdita's passivity which the Shepherd rebukes before the pastoral festivities begin:

> You are retired,
> As if you were a feasted one, and not
> The hostess of the meeting.   (IV, 4)

and Perdita herself rejects passivity in her answer, later, to Camillo's complimentary remark that, if he were one of her flock, he would 'leave grazing . . . and only live by gazing': she replies that if he did he would soon starve.

The final movement of the play is again one of mutuality: when Hermione's statue comes alive, Paulina urges the dumbstruck Leontes into action:

> Nay, present your hand.
> When she was young you woo'd her; now in age
> Is she become the suitor?   (V, 3)

Hermione embraces Leontes and speaks to him, as he receives and embraces her: she moves from stone to active, responsive life.

*   *   *

The dynamic fusion of active and passive in mutual relationship, as it can be traced in the Last Comedies, is an image of human behaviour which grows directly from the preoccupations we have explored throughout a number of plays. In *The Tempest*, this reciprocity in relationship is related closely to the chief concerns of the play. The theme of *The Tempest* is that men are not wholly active, shapers of their individual lives, nor wholly passive, parts of a larger design in which they are merely manipulated objects; human life is in some way an interpenetration of the two. Men shape and are shaped, moving freely within a precise design; because they are neither wholly subjects nor wholly objects, value is neither fully conferred nor fully intrinsic, but again at some point of fusion between the two. Human spontaneity must be contained within a pattern of responsibility, and the two are fused when men make this pattern their own, living it authentically; in this way, too, personal and social can be seen as aspects of a single life. The interpenetration of freedom and precision is also one of mercy and justice, loving and wisdom. Finally, the fusion of personal and social can be seen in the fact that a man finds himself only within the community; he comes into living contact with himself through his living contact with others. Yet he is not simply what others make him, a created reflection of other men's judgements, subject to the flux of their response; he has an identity which is bound up with his established place in society, and it is this real identity, objectively determined, that he finds through others and makes his own.

The Tempest is the only Shakespearian play to observe the dramatic Unities, and it does so for a purpose. The unity of the play lies ultimately in the unity of Prospero's design, the singleness of his action, and the dramatic Unities are meant to reinforce this fact; the whole play is one action, extended in space and time, unified and controlled by Prospero and yet in some sense with an organically developing life of its own. The structure of the play itself, in other words, is an image of its concerns: the action is both Prospero's personal self-expressive act, spontaneously growing and yet rationally controlled, and a record of objective, public events. The fusion of personal and social, spontaneous and rationally responsible, is there in the very form of the drama.

Prospero's unified design has a precedent in the plan of the Duke in *Measure for Measure*. In that play, the complexity of situation and character was contained and controlled within an overall singleness of action, and this sense of unity was expressed powerfully in the idea of a single action which accomplished a number of different ends: the Duke's interchanging of Isabella and Mariana was typical of this. The same relation between an individual act and a whole society is there in the Last Comedies, as we have seen in *The Winter's Tale*; Leontes's personal madness has multiple effects:

> Be certain what you do, sir, lest your justice
> Prove violence, in the which three great ones suffer,
> Yourself, your queen, your son.   (II, 1)

The relation of an individual act to a whole design can be seen in a different way in Perdita. Perdita is characterised, in the pastoral scene, as a girl whose acts are perfectly achieved:

> Each your doing,
> So singular in each particular,
> Crowns what you are doing in the present deeds,
> That all your acts are queens.   (IV, 4)

Each of her single acts seems perfect, a complete self-expression, and yet all her acts are part of a design, each followed by another. This is why the dance is a perfect image of Perdita, for a dance is a progression of achieved individual movements, linked into a whole pattern; she dances 'featly', as she does everything. Perdita seems perfectly achieved in herself, and yet at the same time her actions point outwards to something beyond her:

> . . . nothing she does or seems
> But smacks of something greater than herself,
> Too noble for this place.   (IV, 4)

In *The Tempest*, Prospero's individual acts are also perfectly and gracefully achieved, spontaneously executed by Ariel, but they gain ultimate meaning only in relation to the whole project which we see 'gather to a head' throughout the play under his control. It is in relation to this project that the human beings in the play move, acting freely to an extent, yet shaped by its limits. To be truly oneself is to avoid the conditions of both slavery and individualism: of total passivity within a design, brute objective being, and an exploiting subjectivity which resists integration into any pattern.

The theme of unity is dominant in the play. It is the virtue of compassion, of feeling with another, that immediately characterises Miranda: 'O I have suffered/With those that I saw suffer!' (I, 2).   When Prospero begins to tell Miranda their mutual history, she remembers that when she was a child she had four or five women who attended on her; the fact is reminiscent of the centring of the court of *The Winter's Tale* on Mamillius, on the young child as a living focus of

unity, several bound up in a single concern.* Opposites
are resolved into unity in Prospero's reply to Miranda's
question as to whether it was foul play or blessedness
which brought them from Milan: he says it was both.
This image of two-in-one is echoed in Ferdinand's
description of the music he hears when wandering on the
island:

> . . . This music crept by me up on the waters,
> Allaying both their fury and my passion
> With its sweet air . . .   (I, 2)

The music accomplishes two ends simultaneously,
soothing both Ferdinand and the storm, and the idea of
a double movement resolved within a single action is
continued in Ferdinand's words:

> . . . thence I have follow'd it,
> Or it hath drawn me rather.   (I, 2)

Following and being drawn, acting and being acted on,
seem part of a single condition.

Ariel's description to Prospero of his activity on the
ship reflects a similar sense of singleness and variety:

> . . . Sometimes I'd divide,
> And burn in many places; on the topmast,
> The yards, and bowsprit, would I flame distinctly,
> Then meet and join.   (I, 2)

With Ariel, the interplay of unity and diffusion reflects
an interplay of freedom and precision: he is purely
fluid, invisible to human eye, dismaying and confusing

---

* Cf. Cymbeline's comment on the unity achieved at the end of *Cymbeline*: '. . . the countercharge/Is several in all'   (V, 5).

human beings with his ubiquity and disguises, and yet
he is simultaneously within the control of Prospero,
carrying out his commands with an exactness which is
emphasised; he has performed his labours 'to every
article', 'exactly', 'to th'syllable'. Ariel fuses active and
passive, subject and object: he is bound within the limits
of Prospero's plan, but within these limits moves freely.
He finds scope for his own self-expression in executing
his master's orders, but he has not fully authenticated
his bondage: there is still a tension in him between his
freedom and his responsibility to Prospero, a tension
which his master recognises and finally eases in allowing
him his freedom.

Caliban has not authenticated his bondage at all; he is
a slave, a brute object in Prospero's design. His promise
to show Stephano the beauties of the island is an image
of the interplay of active and passive:

> I prithee let me bring thee where crabs grow;
> And I with my long nails will dig thee pig-nuts;
> Show thee a jay's nest, and instruct thee how
> To snare the nimble marmoset; I'll bring thee
> To clust'ring filberts, and sometimes I'll get thee
> Young scamels from the rock. Wilt thou go with me?   (II, 2)

Caliban's promises fall into two kinds: those which
involve acting on behalf of Stephano, and those which
involve bringing him to the point where he can act for
himself. Caliban will dig him pig-nuts and fetch scamels,
but show him, passively, crabs, filberts and the jay's
nest. Instructing him how to snare marmosets is a
fusion of the two: Caliban will actively show Stephano
how to do something for himself.

But generally Caliban is completely passive, and he

expresses himself almost entirely in passive terms. Cursing is a typical mode of speech with him because it is a wish to see another passively afflicted, as he sees himself:

> As wicked dew as e'er my mother brush'd
> With raven's feather from unwholesome fen
> Drop on you both! A south-west blow on ye
> And blister you all o'er!   (I, 2)

He is set upon and bitten by apes, pricked by hedge-hogs, wounded by adders. He thinks constantly in terms of things dropping from heaven: Stephano, he thinks, has fallen from the moon, and he wishes infections to fall on Prospero from the clouds in the same way that he wishes the sky to drop riches on himself. He is not prepared to murder Prospero himself, only to set others on to do it.

Antonio, by contrast, not only incites Sebastian to murder Alonso, but is quite prepared to do the deed himself. Antonio is the exact opposite of Caliban: he is a completely active man, ruthlessly individualist, creating his own fortunes and his own values. He is an exploiter, concerned with reducing other men to objects; before he supplanted Prospero, he says, Prospero's servants were his fellows: now they are his men. He has full confidence in his ability to manipulate the others after murdering Alonso:

> . . . For all the rest,
> They'll take suggestion as a cat laps milk;
> They'll tell the clock to any business that
> We say befits the hour.   (II, 1)

Antonio resembles Prospero in his spontaneity of action; there is no hesitation in his control, no breakdown between impulse and execution: the steel which will kill the king is 'obedient' to his purpose, and the conscience which troubles Sebastian does not deflect him:

> . . . twenty consciences
> That stand 'twixt me and Milan, candied be they
> And melt, ere they molest!   (II, 1)

He will allow nothing to intervene between his intention and his action: he will execute his plan exactly, without hindrance. He is ruthlessly spontaneous: he tells Sebastian that he will teach him 'how to *flow*'. In both his precision and his spontaneity, Antonio is ironically close to Prospero. Antonio sees conscience as a purposeless impediment, treating it with the same impatience with which he responds to Gonzalo. To him, Gonzalo is a 'spendthrift of his tongue', prating 'amply and unnecessarily': he squanders in words the energy which should be reserved for action. Prospero, too, has this precision, an exactness in fulfilling his purposes: he controls his agents rigorously, demanding precise and immediate performance of his instructions. His long account of his history to Miranda at the beginning of the play is important only in so far as it is an essential preparation for the 'present business': otherwise the story would be 'most impertinent'. At the end of the play he tells Ariel that, if the offenders are penitent, 'The sole drift of (his) purpose doth extend/Not a frown further'. His design is calculated to precision, and carried out spontaneously, without deflection.

The difference between the spontaneity of Antonio

and that of Prospero is similar to the difference between Angelo and the Duke in *Measure for Measure*. Angelo and Antonio, like Coriolanus, are able to be spontaneous, accurate in their self-expression in action, simply because they exclude the kind of complex considerations of responsibility to others which might impede this spontaneity. The Duke and Prospero, on the other hand, achieve a spontaneity of action which takes account of complexities, which is socially responsible. Antonio has no care for others at all: his contempt for Gonzalo's long-windedness is not only the contempt of the active for the inactive man, but an incapacity to respond to the kind of human richness which expresses itself in sheer excess. Antonio has the precision of an automaton; the measure of the exactness of relation between his purpose and action is the measure of his inability to love, his incapacity for gratuitous action. Prospero, by contrast, combines precision and love: with him, the exactness of relation between his purpose and action does not become the exactness of revenge in human relationships, but finds expression in a kind of justice which interpenetrates with mercy, gratuitous forgiveness. His singleness of action is not deflected; his intentions are exactly achieved, but not at the expense of an awareness of complex human failing and responsibility.* Prospero achieves for the others in the play his own fusion of spontaneity and aware responsibility: he orchestrates the individual, clashing and combining wills into a harmony within which they can find fulfilment and identity in terms of an awareness of others.

Gonzalo, in his description of his ideal common-

---

* The idea of an action being deflected from its purpose is there in the first scene of the play, where the courtier's 'mar' the sailors' labour.

wealth, misses the synthesis towards which the play is moving. He sees the value of spontaneous common growth, but lacks a sense of the necessary interaction of this spontaneity with active reasoning and creating:

> All things in common nature should produce
> Without sweat or endeavour. Treason, felony,
> Sword, pike, knife, gun, or need of any engine,
> Would I not have; but nature should bring forth,
> Of its own kind, all foison, all abundance,
> To feed my innocent people.   (II, 1)

Gonzalo has a deep sense of a common, organic life in which men are rooted, and this is valuable when placed against the cynicism of Antonio, who can understand action only as individual; but the passivity of Gonzalo's vision (he sees all men as idle in this utopia) is its inadequacy. Somehow, this spontaneous life must be fused with an active human shaping, with sweat and endeavour; there must be a reciprocity of active and passive, of a common, sustaining design and individual creativity.

This kind of fusion is reflected in Francisco's description, shortly before Gonzalo's speech, of Ferdinand swimming for shore from the wrecked ship:

> Sir, he may live;
> I saw him beat the surges under him,
> And ride upon their backs; he trod the water,
> Whose enmity he flung aside, and breasted
> The surge most swoln that met him; his bold head
> 'Bove the contentious waves he kept, and oared
> Himself with his good arms in lusty stroke
> To th'shore, that o'er his wave-worn basis bowed,
> As stooping to relieve him.   (II, 1)

Here the relationship between man and Nature is dialectical, a dynamic interaction; in swimming a man is actively creating and shaping the current which sustains him, flinging aside the waves so that they may return to buoy him up. Both Ferdinand and the ocean are simultaneously active and passive: the mutual interaction is one between art and Nature, individual shaping and a creating, sustaining context. It is the reciprocity of art and nature in Polixenes's speech to Perdita in the pastoral scene of *The Winter's Tale*, an image of the whole relationship in the Last Comedies between person and society.

This mutually creative relationship is mirrored above all in the union of Miranda and Ferdinand. Prospero's words when the couple first meet suggest this mutuality: they have 'chang'd eyes', and 'are both in either's pow'rs' (I, 2). Prospero lays a task on Ferdinand so that the labour he must perform to win Miranda will make her all the more valuable. She is, in fact, intrinsically valuable, and it is to this intrinsic merit that Ferdinand responds when he first meets her; but this natural fitness will be fused, through Prospero's action, with a humanly created and conferred value, as Ferdinand comes to estimate Miranda even more highly through the work which he does for her. The two kinds of value, intrinsic and created, which we saw in *Troilus and Cressida* as mutually antagonistic, are here resolved into unity: Miranda is valuable both in herself, and in relation to the energy which Ferdinand expends over her. Similarly, the task of chopping logs, which to Ferdinand is in itself odious, becomes delightful because of its context, since it is done for Miranda's sake:

> The mistress which I serve quickens what's dead,
> And makes my labours pleasures.   (III, 1)

A task which has no intrinsic value becomes precious through a human context.

Miranda is sad that Ferdinand should have to labour, and offers to carry the logs herself, but Ferdinand refuses indignantly. Each hates the idea of the other labouring without being able to share in the task and make it mutual. Prospero reduces Ferdinand to the status of a slave, and Miranda wants to take his slavery on herself to save him. But what is really needed for salvation is the mutual bondage and mutual freedom of the love-relationship, where each can find equality through being bound to the other. Miranda and Ferdinand offer themselves to each other as slaves, and through this mutual slavery, precisely because it is mutual, they can find equality and freedom. Ferdinand says he will be slave to his own heart, which has flown to Miranda's service: in serving her he will be serving himself. Miranda declares that she will be Ferdinand's servant even though he denies her permission to be his 'fellow'. Ferdinand then takes Miranda, not as his servant, but as his mistress, and she takes him at the same time as her husband; Ferdinand accepts the status of husband 'with a heart as willing/As bondage e'er of freedom' (III, 1). Prospero's words express the sense of balance and equality in this union:

> Fair encounter
> Of two most rare affections! Heavens rain grace
> On that which breeds between 'em!   (III, 1)

The giving and receiving of the love-relationship will

be simultaneous, as Miranda's timid account of her own inadequacy suggests: she weeps at her unworthiness,

> . . . that dare not offer
> What I desire to give, and much less take
> What I shall die to want.   (III, 1)

It is this mutual exchange which forms the basis of relationship; Miranda's desire for Ferdinand (he is the first man she has ever sighed for) and his love for her establishes a bond which contrasts with the action of Caliban in trying to rape Miranda. To rape is to ignore mutuality: the partners are respectively merely active and merely passive. Through the mutuality of her relationship with Ferdinand, Miranda can come to know herself. She has no knowledge of other women, and thus no capacity to arrive at self-knowledge by comparison; but through Ferdinand's response she can come to self-awareness, making him the glass in which she finds herself and the world reflected.*

The relationship of Miranda and Ferdinand is one of reciprocal giving and receiving, but reciprocity in itself is not sufficient: it must be fertile, must 'breed', otherwise it can become an enclosed circle. This inbred, dangerous kind of reciprocity is a constant image in the play: it occurs in Miranda's description of the storm at sea:

---

* Caliban, who parallels Miranda in many ways, comes to know himself when Prospero first arrives on the island, through *language*. Previously he did not know his own meaning, but the language which Prospero taught him makes his experience intelligible to *himself* as well as to others. Here, as in *Measure for Measure*, language is a creative force, the symbol of the public world through which a man becomes himself.

> The sky, it seems, would pour down stinking pitch,
> But that the sea, mounting to th' welkin's cheek,
> Dashes the fire out.   (I, 2)

This is stalemate, not creative interchange; it is echoed later, in Prospero's account of their desertion at sea:

> There they hoist us,
> To cry to th' sea, that roar'd to us; to sigh
> To th'winds, whose pity, sighing back again,
> Did us but loving wrong.   (I, 2)

Circularity of this kind can be physical: the 'foul witch Sycorax' grew, with age and envy, into a hoop; Prospero threatens to manacle Ferdinand's neck and feet together. Caliban returns in curses the language which Prospero has taught him: again, this is an instance of the danger of circularity, of a sterile give-and-take. The union of Miranda and Ferdinand, by contrast, will be physically fruitful; provided their love is contained within the public sanction and ritual of marriage, heaven will let fall 'sweet aspersions' to 'make the contract grow'. In this last phrase, the fusion of public form and personal spontaneity, of 'contract' and 'grow', is part of the whole synthesis of the play. A true love-relationship must be open, public, rooted in a community; the private act, as Prospero warns Ferdinand, will be barren.

This fusion of public form and personal spontaneity is the meaning of the interpenetration of justice and mercy which Prospero achieves at the end of the play. As in *Measure for Measure*, there must be a public reckoning, a precise settling of accounts, but this is done within the larger context of a gratuitous forgiveness, a free bestowal of love. There is measure for mea-

sure, a restoration of what was lost, physical punishment and discomfort for some of the offenders. But
out of this precise settling a new, creative life can grow;
justice is not inbred, turned in on itself in a barren
settling of scores, but is, instead, the essential condition
for the new life of love to take root.

*   *   *

'Grace' and 'virtue' are recurrent terms in the Last
Comedies, and they can be useful as ways of summaris-
ing what we have said already about these plays. Grace,
for the Christian, means that personal authenticating of
the law which binds together the community, in a way
that makes it natural and spontaneous to act responsibly;
to have grace is to make the law part of one's own life
so that one's most authentic self-expression is in terms
of others, in terms of a society. Virtue is the habit of
goodness, good actions spontaneously done without
hesitation; it is what Hamlet urges Gertrude to at the
end of his encounter with her in Act III, Scene 4:

> Refrain to-night;
> And that shall lend a kind of easiness
> To the next abstinence; the next more easy;
> For use almost can change the stamp of nature,
> And either curb the devil, or throw him out,
> With wondrous potency.

Virtue is 'a kind of easiness', good action done without
labour or reflection; it is the opposite of an external
conformity to law, a sense of law as a necessary but
repressive force, restricting full self-expression. To be
in a condition of grace is to find full authenticity only

within law, as full identity is found only within relationships. Grace therefore effects a fusion of personal and social; it heals the dislocation between public and private, as it heals the gap between impulse and execution. In *The Tempest*, Ariel performs Prospero's commands at a word: his closeness to his master is an image of spontaneity, of a fluent continuity between conception and action. When law ceases to be authentic, instinctive, spontaneity either breaks down, as it does with the Greeks in *Troilus and Cressida*, where action is strangled in reflection, or becomes a disruptive, irresponsible force, self-expression without responsibility. In the Last Comedies, art, as well as grace, is used as an image of spontaneity: art as a fluent embodiment of impulse into action, as the closest responsiveness between human consciousness and the objective world, personal and social.

The synthesis of personal and social is expressed, as we have seen, in the whole action of these plays. To Gonzalo, the plot of *The Tempest* is a 'maze'; to Prospero it is a 'project'. To be able to see individual character and action as part of a larger design is to see the necessary interpenetration of active and passive, freedom and limitation, subject and object, value as created and value as intrinsic. Human life moves at the point of fusion of all these alternatives; to fall on either side of the synthesis of which these dichotomies are separate aspects, is to fail in different ways. In the Last Comedies, Shakespeare explores this synthesis, moving towards a reconciliation of the qualities which in earlier plays were incompatible; in these plays, attitudes which were previously locked in conflict become creatively interactive, forming a new reality, wedding the merits of spontaneous, creative living with the value of a common, responsible way of life. Whether this kind of exploration can be done only within a Christian context, whether grace and virtue must be accepted in a specific sense, remains controversial. But to come to the Last Comedies from the other plays is to see them facing problems which are of common concern, and the exploration itself is perhaps ultimately more important than the specialised connotations of the terms in which it is done.

A Note on *Timon of Athens*

Timon of Athens is a disturbingly unsuccessful play, crude and unbalanced like its hero; but the nature of the imbalance in Timon himself can be usefully related to aspects of what we have seen in *Measure for Measure* and the Last Comedies. Timon begins as a man lavish in his giving to others, and then swings as a result of ingratitude into extreme misanthropy. It is worth noting the quality of his lavishness:

> Plutus, the god of gold,
> Is but his steward; no meed but he repays
> Sevenfold above himself; no gift to him
> But breeds the giver a return exceeding
> All use of quittance. (I, 1)

There is a destructive quality in this, in spite of the generosity: Timon's liberality overwhelms, reducing other givers and their gifts to nothing beside itself. It soon becomes evident that Timon does not know how to receive, in spite of his ability to give, and that his giving is in fact a way of forestalling and cancelling the giving of others. When Ventidius wants to return to Timon some talents he borrowed from him, Timon refuses to take them because he sees this return as destroying the meaning of the gift:

> O, by no means,
> Honest Ventidius! You mistake my love;
> I gave it freely ever; and there's none
> Can truly say he gives, if he receives. (I, 2)

Timon has not learnt that, to quote E. M. Forster, it is more blessed to receive than to give, and that it is best to be able to do both simultaneously. He rejects the reciprocity of giving and receiving, and thus rejects relationship; his refusal to receive belittles givers as surely as does Apemantus's firm resolve to give nothing to anybody, ever. When Lucius gives Timon four milk-white horses, Timon responds:

> I shall accept them fairly. Let the presents
> Be worthily entertain'd.   (I, 2)

His gesture of generosity to the horses caps Lucius's generosity in giving them. Timon refuses to be anything but a source: he will not make himself the object of another's kindness.

The lack of reciprocity in his giving is emphasised in his remark after the masque which he puts on to entertain his guests: he thanks the ladies who took part in the masque for their efforts, and says that they have entertained him 'with (his) own device'. The circularity of this is familiar and significant: for Timon, the act of giving is its own reward. At this point, the circularity which we have seen in other plays reaches its final, subtle irony: now it is the actual act of giving and responding to others which has become merely a kind of self-expression, a self-definition. It is part of the falseness of this giving that it is completely gratuitous: Timon gives anything to anyone, without regard for intrinsic merit or particular circumstance. Since giving, for him, is self-satisfying, done for its own sake, he can ignore actual values and qualities. He is able to accept the snarling criticism of Apemantus, and still be generous to him, precisely because his generosity is a kind of abstraction, divorced from considerations of context:

APEMANTUS Let me stay at thine apperil, Timon.
  I come to observe; I give thee warning on't.
TIMON I take no heed of thee. Th'art an Athenian, therefore
  welcome. (I, 2)

His giving is a kind of detachment: the less heed he takes of people, the more generous he can be. It is a lavishness which cancels itself out: to give to all is equivalent to giving to none, striking value out of giving. Timon ignores intrinsic merits, conferring gifts indiscriminately as the impulse takes him. The Poet's description of his poem to Timon, in the first scene, also describes Timon s behaviour:

> My free drift
> Halts not particularly, but moves itself
> In a wide sea of tax. (I, 1)

Timon ignores his steward Flavius's urging to plan and reckon his expenditure, and bankrupts himself: his generosity is literally self-destroying. The excessive misanthropy he shows when his fortunes change is merely the reverse of the extreme lavishness he showed before: like this, it ignores particularities, expresses itself in wildly general terms, and is a projected egoism. When he meets Alcibiades, who is on his way to attack Athens, he wishes him success, and hopes he will finally destroy himself:

> The gods confound them all in thy conquest!
> And thee after, when thou hast conquer'd! (IV, 3)

This has the same structure as Timon's earlier response to Lucius's giving of horses: in both cases, Timon wants the final victory, refusing to be on inferior or even equal terms with another. He sympathises with Alcibiades's aims and then objectifies him too, wishing for his destruction along with the fall of Athens.*

The relation of this quality in Timon to *Measure for Measure* and the Last Comedies is important. For Timon's lavish giving has something of the quality of the forgiveness which we saw in those plays; forgiveness, too, is a gratuitous giving, largely independent of the merits of the receiver, a free act and therefore in a sense an indiscriminate one, done for its own sake. Forgiveness embraces all men, and thus cancels out any strict scheme of intrinsic merit, like Timon's giving. What the exploration in this play does is to underline the importance of the fact that, in *Measure for Measure* and the Last Comedies, forgiveness works within the context of justice, of a measure of exact and reciprocal reckoning of particular accounts. Without this firm basis, forgiveness could degenerate into the excess which Timon reveals. *Timon of Athens* does in fact interpolate a scene about mercy and justice: in Act III Scene 5 Alcibiades pleads with the first senator for the life of a friend who killed a man in just anger, and the senator refuses to admit this consideration, stressing the universal evil of killing regardless of the merits of the concrete situation. In ignoring the justice of the

---

* Notice, however, that Timon's rantings against *gold* show a reversal of his previous commitment to giving as self-satisfying; gold is a medium of human communication, and those who worship it as a thing-in-itself make precisely the mistake which Timon made earlier, in making the act of giving an end in itself.

killing, the senator is merciless in his condemnation; for Alcibiades, to recognise the element of justice in the act is to be merciful:

> To kill, I grant, is sin's extremest gust;
> But, in defence, by mercy, 'tis most just. (III, 5)

The co-existence of 'just' and 'mercy' in the same line points to the kind of fusion which *Measure for Measure* tries to achieve. The senator's rejection of the claims of precise reckoning stands with Timon's similar rejection, as the dangerous extreme of a free impartial response which, when qualified, is valuable.

Conclusion

THE themes and problems in Shakespeare examined in these chapters are clearly not the whole of what is there to be discovered in the plays, but it is equally true that no particular selection of aspects of a writer's work can ever be wholly random. I have looked at Shakespeare mainly in terms of what I see as one major crisis in his work—the tension between spontaneous life and society—because this seems to me a crisis which, in the light of our own experience, we are especially well-placed to appreciate and understand. This understanding, of course, can never be a mechanical 'updating' of Shakespeare, the tagging on to a specifically Shakespearian study of a few remarks about our own time; nor is the understanding possible because the problems are 'universal', applying to Shakespeare's time and our own in a similar way. Our own understanding of this crisis is a particular one, part of a response to a whole social condition, and it cannot be separated from this context without being reduced to an abstraction. The relation between our own experience and Shakespeare's is made in the critical response to the plays and the problems they present; if we locate specific patterns of ideas and respond to them, it is because we are shaped by our own experience to see significance there, rather than elsewhere.

Our own understanding of the tension between spontaneity and society arises within the context of the society and the cultural tradition which we have received from the last century. It is therefore immediately a detailed problem and a detailed understanding: the problem comes through to us as lived experience, not as formula. It is the experience of an industrial society which shapes the problem for us, and we read Shakespeare through this experience, finding that the language we use to describe his responses is the language we have inherited from the tradition of response to that society. In this Conclusion I want to look briefly at the way experience of the problems we have seen in Shakespeare has been formulated in our own time. It seems necessary to do this, not just to show how the same problems have stayed with us, in a changed form, but to make the preceding study of Shakespeare fully comprehensible by an account of the contemporary experience in terms of which it is written. We can best give such an account by looking briefly at a few nineteenth-century figures, and then seeing how, more recently, the problem has presented itself in terms of an argument about the nature of socialism.

In his essay *The Function of Criticism at the Present Time*, Matthew Arnold argued that one of the chief sicknesses of Victorian society was that men were too ready to rush into social action without first of all stopping to think and criticise freely:

The Englishman has been called a political animal, and he values what is political and practical so much that ideas easily become objects of dislike in his eyes, and thinkers 'miscreants', because ideas and thinkers have rashly meddled with politics and practice. This would be all very well if the dislike and neglect confined themselves to ideas transported out of their own sphere, and meddling rashly with practice; but they are inevitably extended

to ideas as such, and to the whole life of intelligence; practice is
everything, a free play of the mind is nothing.[1]

The position is a familiar one with Arnold: he argues
it most notably in *Culture and Anarchy*, where the emphasis, as here, is on the development of a full and
cultivated humanity which will not easily be side-tracked
by ill-considered calls to action. The really urgent need,
he says there, is 'to lay in a stock of light for our difficulties'; the best way of discovering some lasting truth
is 'not so much by lending a hand to our friends and
countrymen in their actual operations for the removal
of certain definite evils, but rather in getting our friends
and countrymen to seek culture, to let their consciousness play freely around their present operations and the
stock notions on which they are founded . . .'. This is
not to advocate the complete desertion of action; the
need is to find 'some sounder basis of knowledge on
which to act', to create a framework out of which really
fruitful reforms will grow.

Arnold's position, as it stands, seems unexception-
able, the response of an open and sensitive man to a
society blinded by its own concern with the 'machinery'
of specific legislation and activity. But a protest against
ill-considered action can slide, under pressure, into
what begins to look like a protest against action itself;
it is this which characterises much of *The Function of
Criticism*. Arnold begins by emphasising the importance, at a literary level, of criticism, as a factor second-
ary to actual creative writing but essential for the genera-
tion of a living context of ideas; but when the discussion moves on to society, criticism starts to assume pre-
cedence over action. Arnold begins by noting and dis-

approving an English characteristic – a 'mania' for the
political and practical – and goes on to develop what becomes effectively an attack on politics and practice
themselves, as inherently crude and inferior. Criticism
seeks out the best that is thought and known, 'irrespec-
tively of practice, politics, and everything of the kind';
it refuses 'to lend itself to any of those ulterior, political,
practical considerations about ideas, which plenty of
people will be sure to attach to them . . .'. The practical
man, Arnold asserts, is incapable of 'fine distinction',
and he underlines the point by a skilful use of emotive
language in describing the temptations of action:

> The rush and roar of practical life will always have a dizzying
> and attracting effect upon the most collected spectator, and tend
> to draw him into its vortex . . .[2]

What has happened to Arnold's attitude to action by
the end of the essay is exactly what, in the first quotation, he described as happening to the English attitude
to ideas: a specific judgement on misplaced action has
slid into a contempt for action as such.

The same kind of attitude to actual political involvement emerges from *Culture and Anarchy*. Arnold
caricatures this involvement as an interest in 'church
rates' and marriage laws, and points to Cornell University as an instance of this misdirected activity: it seems
'calculated to produce miners, or engineers, or architects,
not sweetness and light'. Sweetness and light, clearly,
have nothing to do with the actual processes by which
men live together, processes involving mines and build-
ings; they are beyond these, inward, untainted by sordid
detail. Arnold does not always take this position – his
general definition of 'culture' takes account of a whole

way of life, of feelings and institutions simultaneously —
but this emphasis can often be felt. The suggestion,
at times, is that the real life of a society is the interior
one, of poetry and ideas; concern with actual issues is
narrow-minded and superficial.

The strength and weakness implicit in Arnold's
approach are so close to each other that judgement is
often confused; the line between criticising particular
kinds of action, and despising action itself, is thin
enough for one attitude to be easily mistaken for the
other. What Arnold affirms, against the cruder reformers
of his time, is a deep and personal sense of the humane,
and it is from this standpoint that he attacks the merely
mechanical. But 'mere machinery' comes near at times
to including almost the whole of social reality; the fine,
flexible life which the 'free play of thought' exempli-
fies opposes itself to social institutions as such. 'Human
thought, which makes all institutions, inevitably saps
them, resting only in that which is absolute and eternal.'[3]
Social action, rather than shaping an interior culture,
becomes merely an implementation of what has already
been inwardly formed through reflection: a putting of
culture (in the interior sense) into operation. What is
missing in this scheme is a sense of interaction between
idea and action, between a society's quality of 'inward'
life and its actual structures. A whole culture does not
in *fact* reflect on itself, establish some basis of value,
and then enact this in institutional terms; it explores
itself *through* action, determining a quality of life in the
real processes of living. Action and quality of life shape
each other, and a division of 'interior' and 'external' is
possible only in abstraction. Arnold failed at times to see
this, because the free, spontaneous life which he valued

contained within it elements hostile to the whole idea of complex, social institutions, institutions which shape, as well as manifest, a quality of life. In his essay *Equality*, for instance, what looks like a radical insight into the nature of equality suddenly shows itself as a quite traditional judgement:

> Whether he mix with high or low, the gentleman feels himself in a world not alien or repulsive, but a world where people make the same sort of demands upon life, in things of this sort, which he himself does.[4]

The image of the gentleman at ease in his club among personal friends is offered as relevant to the complex institutional problems of a developing democracy.

Arnold's work reveals a general difficulty in Victorian social thinking: the difficulty that the quality of life in the name of which a particular society is criticised takes on a generalised hostility to politics, institution, action, so that free, personal expression and social forms are at odds. Arnold's attitude to action in *The Function of Criticism at the Present Time* is like that of the scholar in Browning's poem *The Grammarian's Funeral*, who rather than explore life in the process of living it, wants first to learn all about it and then live it. The problem is as significant for Browning, in a different way, as it is for Arnold: Browning's poems explore the experience of creating value in the process of living, through an intensity of energy: the Trojan position in contrast to Arnold's Greek conception, if one may put it that way.* In a poem like *The Statue and*

---

* Newman's idea of Christian faith as a commitment which becomes fully real only in the process of being lived is also significant of this attitude.

the Bust, it is a lived intensity which confers value: even when the prize is small, Browning urges,

> Stake your counter as boldly every whit,
> Venture as warily, use the same skill,
> Do your best, whether winning or losing it,
>
> If you choose to play!—is my principle.
> Let a man contend to the uttermost
> For his life's set prize, be it what it will!

In *My Last Duchess*, it is the Duchess's cancellation of accepted values, her equal prizing of her husband's ancient name and a bough of cherries, which causes the Duke's annoyance. Browning explores one kind of solution to the problem of action, the solution of Tennyson in *Ulysses*; but it is a solution which can only, ultimately, be anti-social, an individualist self-definition beyond the edges of society.

The difficulty occurs again in the work of Carlyle, and here the growing tension between spontaneity and society follows the contour of a chronological development. Carlyle begins, in his early work, by making an analysis of industrialism in terms of its crippling of spontaneous life – what he calls 'Dynamism'. A mechanical society is seen to be destroying natural energies: men have grown mechanical in both head and hand. 'Mechanism has now struck its roots down into man's most intimate, primary sources of conviction; and is thence sending up, over his whole life and activity, innumerable stems – fruit-bearing and poison-bearing.' Yet Carlyle, in his criticism of mechanism, merely external ordering, did not reject social institutions as such. He recognised that to do this was as symptomatic of sickness as to be concerned merely with mechanical arrangements: it would encourage 'idle, visionary, and impracticable courses'. He saw that the inward and spontaneous must work closely in terms of social forms:

> To define the limits of these two departments of man's activity (dynamic and mechanical), which work into one another, and by means of one another, so intricately and inseparably, were by its nature an impossible attempt . . . it seems clear enough that only in the right co-ordination of the two, and the vigorous forwarding of *both*, does our true line of action lie.[5]

Carlyle fought against 'mere political arrangement', but he saw too, at this stage, that what was wrong was a matter of human institutions as well as a falsity of feeling. In *Chartism*, the concern with institutions is clear: Carlyle rejects the superficial formulas about Chartism, looking below the surface and seeing particular issues in relation to a deep-seated disease, but the penetration of the surface is not an implied contempt for it, a rejection of the actual. His evaluation of the Poor Law is careful and detailed, a reasoned and committed response. Much of Carlyle's early work shows this balance between a complex awareness of the actual issues, and the sense of a whole quality of life to which the issues must be related.

But Carlyle, perhaps more than any other nineteenth-century thinker, exposes the paradox implicit in rejecting the actual condition of society from the stand-point of a spontaneous life which it lacks. In the later work, the impatience with a mere tinkering with the surface of society becomes an effective rejection of all constructive action; the habit of penetrating below the superficial response to a whole vision becomes a way of undermining the actual. All practical attempts to fight mechanism become themselves machinery: 'surface' comes to include all actual social life, and this is nothing beside the deep, cosmic life which lies beneath. A statement like 'Sooty Manchester — it too is built on the infinite abysses'[6] cuts both ways: it can intensify a sense of the actual by seeing it in terms of a deeper life; it can also belittle the actual in relation to the vague, awful cosmos which surrounds it. The paradox of Carlyle is that what is rejected along with the 'machinery' of a deadening society is all the available means of changing it; spontaneous life comes to reject practical measure and institution by habit, unable to see these as anything but inferior. As a result, Carlyle is forced back onto the personal feeling, the personal ideal, constructing heroic images in a void. His own recognition that the actual 'goes rotten' when not sustained by the ideal is, when reversed, his own situation: the ideal goes rotten when not sustained by any actual embodiment. The absence of any available way of living as an alternative to industrial capitalist society drives the humane values into an intense abstraction, from which they can find relief only momentarily, in the substitute living which the act of writing offers.

The situation is particularly poignant with Carlyle, because it is not difficult to understand the quality of his response to the actual political developments of his time, and to share his feeling that many of the ways of change available were mechanistic. The man who sees deepest will be the man least able to commit himself freely to kinds of reform which lack the depth of his own insight. It is less easy to see how, with the experience of Carlyle and his tradition to draw on, this can still be advanced as an adequate position today, when the pressures of merely mechanical change are as strong as ever, but where also we have learnt, from the strengths and failures of the tradition, to recognise new ways of going beyond them. Carlyle was right to protest against the mentality which saw the Reform Bill as the millennium; but a millennium can only be reached by actual measures, by specific reforms. He saw in his early work that in an industrial society above all, any distinction between ways of feeling and social institutions is facile, and even in his worst excesses his aim is still the regeneration of a whole society, to establish 'a manlike place and relation in the world' and release the flow of the 'life-fountains'. If he lost sight ultimately of the intricate and inseparable fusion of the 'inward' and the 'external', it is because the pressures of living his values in a vacuum were too strong to prevent abstraction. Carlyle poses the general question: how is spontaneous life to be translated into terms of a whole society without hardening into mechanism? Both Arnold and Carlyle, at their best, were perceptive enough to see that what was demanded was something more than the personal solution which is always one kind of answer. They identified the problem as social, and saw that it could be met only in social terms. To talk about 'personal relationships', in a society where no relationship can be separated off from the whole social reality which institutions shape, is itself a symptom of the disease. Carlyle knew the falsity of a whole society as a personal feeling, in *Signs of the Times*, but he did not there make the mistake of thinking that, because the experience was personally lived, it was *merely* inward, beyond the shaping of social structures.

John Stuart Mill's attempt to reconcile the thinking of Bentham and Coleridge is one, conscious effort towards a synthesis of 'inward' and 'external' in the nineteenth century, but what finally emerges is separation rather than fusion. Mill accepts Bentham's method as a useful means of dealing with the social and institutional side of living: 'It can teach the means of organising and regulating the merely *business* part of the social arrangements'.[7] But Benthamism is inadequate to deal with the 'spiritual interests' of life, and Mill will therefore correct this imbalance by uniting it with Coleridge's thought, which can supply the necessary interior culture of the feelings. Raymond Williams has pointed out how completely intellectualist Mill's method is here: he is trying abstractly to combine what are, when lived, incompatible ways of looking.[8] What Mill ends with, effectively, is two different ethics: one for 'external' living, and one for 'inward' living. Benthamism will take care of the detail of social life, Coleridge will provide the imaginative richness which the utilitarian programme overlooks. This is the breakdown that we saw in the later Carlyle: personal, spontaneous life and 'the ordering of outward circumstances' (as Mill calls it in the *Autobiography*) are quite divorced. For Mill, institutions are not to engage the kind of imaginative responsiveness which the poetry of Wordsworth teaches him to feel; they can be left safely to the Benthamite reformers, as the merely external aspects of society. Ironically, Mill comes nearer to a real sense of the wholeness of inward and external in his account of his early response to Benthamism, in the *Autobiography*: 'It gave unity to my conception of things. I now had opinions; a creed, a doctrine, a philosophy; in one among the best senses of the word, a religion; the inculcation and diffusion of which could be made the principle outward purpose of a life.'[9] Here his response is a living combination of feeling and intellect to a body of thought which offers him simultaneously an interior, religious principle, and an actual engagement in the work of changing society.

Mill is concerned, notably in *On Liberty*, with the necessity of preserving living human energies from the tyranny of a mechanical society:

If it were felt that the free development of individuality is one of the leading essentials of well-being; that it is not only a co-ordinate element with all that is designated by the terms civilisation, instruction, education, culture, but is itself a necessary part and condition of all those things; there would be no danger that liberty should be undervalued, and the adjustment of the boundaries between it and social control would present no extraordinary difficulty. But the evil is, that individual spontaneity is hardly recognised by the common modes of thinking as having any intrinsic worth, or deserving any regard on its own account. The majority, being satisfied with the ways of mankind as they now are (for it is they who make them what they are), cannot comprehend why those ways should not be good enough for everybody; and what is more, spontaneity forms no part of the ideal of the majority of moral and social reformers, but is rather looked on with jealousy, as a troublesome and perhaps rebellious obstruction to the general acceptance of what these reformers, in their own judgement, think would be best for mankind.[10]

'Spontaneity forms no part of the ideal of the majority of moral and social reformers': Mill sees the problem clearly, and without losing balance. The whole of the essay is an exploration of the ways in which real human life can find expression, within an actual society; beliefs and institutions must be renewed, so that they 'connect' with 'the inner life of the human being', but this kind of renewal implies no rejection of social forms themselves. Mill's sense of human energies is rich and powerful, and here at least there is no intellectualism:

> Human nature is not a machine to be built after a model, and set to do exactly the work prescribed for it, but a tree, which requires to grow and develop itself on all sides, according to the tendancy of the inward forces which make it a living thing.[11]

Mill puts the development of authentic life at the centre of his argument: a society must allow men to unfold their real selves, without stunting these selves within false, mechanical categories. Men must not let themselves be dominated by a social pattern, but must authenticate it personally:

> He who lets the world, or his own portion of it, choose his plan of life for him, has no need of any other faculty than the ape-like one of imitation. He who chooses his plan for himself, employs all his faculties. He must use observation to see, reasoning and judgement to foresee, activity to gather materials for decision, discrimination to decide, and when he has decided, firmness and self-control to hold to deliberate decision.[12]

A man must achieve a personal wholeness, not submit blindly to offered social definitions. The emphasis on the free expression of personal energy leads Mill at points into a negative version of society: society as an aggregate of authentic individuals, with the accent on personal authenticity, in isolation from relationship. But although the connection between spontaneous life and social forms still cannot be made in detail in *On Liberty*, the general concern with an actual society is a sign of strength. Mill, in his insistence on a wholeness of self-expression, stands in the tradition which is inherited most notably in our own time by D. H. Lawrence, but he, perhaps more than most thinkers in the tradition, had a shrewd and acute awareness of the problem in its real context, the context of a complex, extending industrial democracy.

It is authenticity, in its deepest sense, which Carlyle is calling for, and in his work the sense of thwarted authentic energies which comes through in Mill finds its most explicit expression. In *Heroes and Hero-worship*, Carlyle demands 'a veracity, a natural spontaneity in forms', and the relation of 'veracity' to spontaneity is vital in his thinking. For Carlyle, a society which cripples spontaneous life is inauthentic, false in the way in which a man who stifles his own deepest instincts is false; Victorian society is not only evil but, in some sense, unreal. He calls for an authentic society, a society whose forms and institutions are a close and living expression of the life of its people. Injustice is not merely wrong but is 'acted untruth'[13]; the French Revolution is the explosive return of a false society to its real self. Carlyle agrees with Mill about the purpose of life: it is 'to unfold your *self*, to work what thing you have the faculty for'[14]; society is false when it denies this kind of authenticity. What is needed is a return to a 'felt indubitable certainty of experience'[15] as a sound basis from which to live and build. This sense of an authentic life from which society has deviated is very strong in Carlyle, but like the cosmic awareness, it can be both a strength and a weakness. On the one hand it can provide a touchstone by which to judge an actual society, a sense of ultimate value around which social criticism can centre; against this, it can merely reinforce the idea that 'real' life is below the surface, beyond the historical accidents, present 'inside' society, waiting for society to rediscover it. If there is an ideal, authentic essence, then the faults of an actual society are merely momentary and unreal; attention is turned from these to the 'eternal verities' which they distortedly reflect. The engaged optimism of *Signs of the Times*, with its simultaneous awareness of complex problems and a dynamism which can resolve them, can become in the later work a detached and empty assertion of cosmic truths which belittles the detailed difficulties of social change.

The sense of society's falsity, in a way suggestive of a deeper distortion than common hypocrisy, is a significant feeling in the nineteenth century, and it comes through powerfully in the later novels of Dickens. In *Little Dorrit* and *Our Mutual Friend*, society is unreal, falsifying, dislocating men from all living touch with truth. This is Little Dorrit's feeling about Italy:

. . . all she saw appeared unreal; the more surprising the scenes, the more they resembled the unreality of her own inner life as she went through its vacant places all day long. The gorges of the Simplon, its enormous depths and thundering waterfalls, the wonderful road, the points of danger where a loose wheel or a faltering horse would have been destruction . . . all a dream – only the mean old Marshalsea a reality.[16]

The Marshalsea in *Little Dorrit*, like the forge and the marshes in *Great Expectations*, becomes a touchstone of reality: the further away from this elemental life one moves, the more unreal life becomes. The movement away is rarely complete: the Marshalsea follows Little Dorrit to Italy as a subcurrent of reality beneath the hollowness; Jo and Magwitch burst into Pip's fashionable London life, as elements from a living past. To live authentically is to be in touch with this rockbottom reality, aware of crime and evil and yet, within this, in close human relationship: the family in the prison, the home near the convict ships. The problem of authentic living is a social problem, as Dickens sees, a question of the possibilities of life which a society can offer; but it presents itself simultaneously as directly personal, a crisis of individual identity. This is so in *Our Mutual Friend*, where the tension between social and spontaneous life is focused within individual characters and becomes a choice of self: Bella Wilfer is torn between the empty values of a bourgeois society and the humane life her father represents; the grinding tension in Bradley Headstone is a struggle to confine his real, passionate self within the limits of the rigid social self which the education system has enforced on him.

But a rockbottom reality is something to build on rather than rest in, and it is this which exposes the limitation in Dickens. In *Little Dorrit*, the movement towards an authentic life is so demanding in its claims on human energy that, when rockbottom is reached and the Marshalsea returned to, the movement outwards can only be a tentative gesture. The end of the novel, as with the end of *Great Expectations*, is to return to the starting-point and know the place for the first time; but how this knowledge of fundamental truth is then to be carried over into positive life is less sure. The authentic

life 'below the surface' of society exposes the deadness
of the conventional world, but the connection between
the qualities of this authentic life and a possible society
cannot be made. The underworld questions society, but
cannot itself offer any lasting alternative. Dickens's
inability to go beyond personal authenticity as a value
in itself is related to his similar inability to go beyond
personal, spontaneous life as an end in itself, in a novel
like *Hard Times*: the image of spontaneous life there is a
circus, something outside the social system, and the
forces which are actually trying to build an alternative
society are dismissed in a caricature.[17] In novels like
Oliver Twist, *Dombey and Son*, and *Bleak House*, the use
of the child as the centre of an indictment of society has
a similar limitation. The child-figure focuses the suffering and vulnerability implicit in society, but its response
is confused and uncomplex, demanding instant, concrete aid as a complete solution to its problems. To use
the child-figure is therefore both to show the suffering
at its most agonising, and, ironically, to evade any complex, long-term and radical response to the problems of
industrial society: the child demands nothing more than
food and love, personally given, and what is generalised
from this action is then merely an ethic of individual
charity which leaves the system unchanged. The child
cannot understand the complex social issues, and it is
easy to make these look abstract and inhuman beside
its immediate, physical need. The child-figure, like the
Marshalsea, can ultimately be a negative response: its
bewilderment is Dickens's own confusion.

Dickens's kind of response still provided the basis
for a great deal of English social thinking at the end of
the nineteenth century, and on into our own time. This

passage from *Towards Democracy*, a long poem by the anarchist poet and social critic Edward Carpenter, shows the influence:

> Stronger than all combinations of Capital, wiser than all the Committees representative of Labour, the simple need and hunger of the human heart.
> Nothing more is needed.
> All the books of political economy ever written, all the proved impossibilities, are of no account.
> The smoke-blackened walls and tall chimneys duly crumble and convey themselves away;
> The falsehood of a gorged and satiated society curls and shrive together like a withered leaf,
> Before the forces which lie dormant in the pale and wistful face of a little child.[18]

This, written in 1882, is recognisably from Carlyle and Dickens, with something of Whitman. The easy contempt for political economy, the juxtaposing of the child and the abstract nouns of Capital and Labour, the sense of a society's falsehood sliding into a satisfying image of society dissolving, as an unreal showpiece —these put Carpenter directly into the tradition, as a minor but very representative figure. What has to be affirmed against the sentiment of this passage is that 'the simple need and hunger of the heart' has to be negotiated, in modern industrial society, in terms of the labour and chimneys and scientific knowledge which are here casually written off; the separation is unreal. But the statement in the poem has all the grand ease of an assured and acceptable conviction: it is clearly part of a conventional wisdom, a popular piety, which expects to be assented to with hardly a thought.

By the time Carpenter came to write, this rejection of institutions had become a traditional gesture.

Carpenter wrote a great deal about society, and his thinking is very much influenced by the anarchism he inherited in a generalised way from Whitman and Tolstoy, and in a more specific form from Kropotkin. The popularity of anarchism in the last years of the nineteenth century in Britain is clearly significant: anarchism is an attempt to make a detailed social programme out of the free spontaneity of men, as individuals or in community, to reconcile social institution and spontaneous life by refining institutions to the point where they can accommodate human spontaneity without distortion. But the emphasis tended to fall, at times, on the spontaneity rather than on social responsibility, and with Carpenter at least, institutions came a long way second:

Of that which exists in the Soul, political freedom and institutions of equality, and so forth, are but the shadows (necessarily thrown); and Democracy in States and Constitutions but the shadow of that which first expresses itself in the glance of the eye or the appearance of the skin. . . . The world travels on – and shall travel on.

A few centuries shall not exhaust the meanings of it. In you and me too, inevitably, its meanings wait their unfolding.

No old laws, precedents, combinations of men or weapons can retard it; no new laws, schemes, combinations, discoveries, can hasten it; but only the new births within the Soul, you and me. . .

When Yes has once been pronounced in that region then the No of millions is nothing at all; then fire, the stake, death, ridicule, and bitter extermination, are of no avail whatever;

When the Ideal has once alighted. . . . When a new desire has declared itself within the human heart, when a fresh plexus is forming among the nerves – then the revolutions of nations are already decided, and histories unwritten are written.[19]

Here the tradition of Arnold and Carlyle meets new influences, in Hegel and Plato and Lamarck, but the final attitude is the same: change is an inward phenomenon, and the movement is from within outwards, from soul to surface. Institutions are simply the crust of society, projected forms which can change only when the inner life has experienced change. Spontaneity is now actively anti-social, in the sense of forestalling all creative human activity to change society: change is an inward, organic process which develops spontaneously, beyond the rational control of men, and no interference with this is possible. The 'No' of millions is nothing beside the will of the interior Life: the fact that this statement occurs in a poem called *Towards Democracy* reflects an interesting political development. Carpenter uses the Lamarckian theory of evolution to underline his point: desire precedes structure, in Lamarck's account of biological evolution, and the same must therefore be true of any social development. We are back with Arnold, but an Arnold reinforced by Hegel: first the Idea, then the embodiment. Carpenter's idea of spontaneity reduces men to passive beings, and society to a temporary configuration on the surface of the infinite.

The spontaneous exfoliation of a society's inner life also reduces particular institutions to insignificance because exfoliation is constant and fluid: no one stage of the unfolding can express the full process, the complete Idea:

Villeins and thralls become piece-men and day-tal men, and

the bondsmen of the land become the bondsmen of Machinery and Capital; the escaped convicts of Labour fit admiringly the bracelets of Wealth round their own wrists. . . .

One skin cast leaves another behind, and that another, and that yet another. . . .'[20]

Carpenter's imagery is dominated by the idea of husks and sheaths falling off from newly formed realities: institutions are continually being created and falling away, as evolution moves beyond them. This gives a relative quality to any particular belief, idea, social form: any social institution is merely a momentarily focused image of the developing inner life of a society, and no total commitment to the actual is therefore possible. Society, as Carpenter sees it, is developing towards some form of socialism, but it would be a mistake to try to describe this form closely, and even this will not be final: the 'husk' of socialist institutions will fall away, as a new reality eventually emerges. Any one stage is limiting, less than the whole, as a single identity is less than the whole:

> I will be the ground underfoot and the common clay;
> The ploughman shall turn me up with his ploughshare. . . .
> The potter shall mould me, running his finger along my
>   running edge. . . .[21]

This is Whitman's influence, of course, but it is part of Carpenter's political attitude: he wants to avoid the restriction of any single definition, any one identity, as he wants to avoid the actual, defining detail of any specific social commitment, keeping himself free and flexible. The 'negative capability' of the Romantic poet and the unconfined spontaneity of the anarchist are aspects of the same sensibility.

Carpenter's actual attitude to contemporary politics is significant of his general stance: he moved freely and with no sense of incongruity amongst all the left-wing bodies of his time – Socialist League, Fabians, anarchists, Labour Party – with no concern for the deep and often bitter differences which divided them. He made this clear in a newspaper article:

A larger heart we want towards each other all through the Labour movement. Such a big thing it is – and is going to be – such innumerable work is to be done, of all sorts and kinds. Burns at his kind, Kier Hardie at his, Nunquam at another, Morris or Kropotkin at another. . . . Criticise each other's work by all means, but don't make the mistake of thinking that because the other man is working at a different part of the *same building* from you that therefore he is working in opposition to you. . . .[22]

The generous common-sense of this is convincing, but the general exhortation – to stop squabbling and take the broad view – is traditionally liberal in a way which Burns and Morris themselves would instantly have seen. For on any actual analysis of left-wing politics in the '80s and '90s, the persuasive metaphor of the single building breaks down; to say of Burns, at this time a militant Marxist, and of Kropotkin, an extreme anarchist, that they are really united beneath their apparent differences, is to show oneself as detached from the complex issues at stake. It is always difficult to make this criticism, because Carpenter's general point is in a way valuable; the line where genuine flexibility becomes vague detachment is always difficult to draw. Carpenter belonged to a tradition of socialism which emphasised that socialism was about human relationships at a time when this was perhaps in danger of being forgotten by other socialists: he insisted always on the inevitably exploratory character of any living socialism, and this has to be set against the weaknesses with which it is so intricately involved.

Carpenter is important because he is in many ways very typical of his time, and an attitude to spontaneity and social institutions can be seen clearly in his work in a way not always possible with more complex thinkers. His socialism is of its period, closely bound up with a belief in art and sexual freedom, Nature and the land, animals and physical health; he was honorary President of the Manchester Vegetarian Society, but ate meat occasionally so as not to be doctrinaire. What is important about this kind of socialism, for all its escapist oddity, is that it is felt as an immediately personal way of life, an experience already available, which is to be extended to others. The lived quality of it has therefore to be weighed against the vagueness of the extension, which is rarely concerned with actual institutions. The same qualities are there in the sexual radicalism of the period, in which Carpenter played a considerable part. The main emphasis of this can be found in Whitman:

It is to the development, identification, and general prevalence of that fervid comradeship . . . that I look for the counterbalance and offset of our materialistic and vulgar American democracy, and for the spiritualisation thereof . . . I say democracy infers such loving comradeship, as its most inevitable twin or counterpart, without which it will be incomplete, in vain, and incapable of perpetuating itself.[23]

Whitman's idea of the new society is of the growth and extension of a web of personal relationships between men: homosexuality as a political force. But what this kind of shared personal life would actually mean, in terms of a complex society, is less clear: the clue, perhaps, is in the words 'counterbalance and offset', which imply that this intense life will be an alternative *within* industrial society rather than the basis of a real social revolution. Sexuality expresses a kind of free and spontaneous life which challenges existing society, but how its energies are to be translated into institutional terms is a problem which is not faced.

The same difficulties arise in the idea of the artist as archetypal of the new society. Carpenter follows Ruskin and Morris in seeing in art the kind of creative power which capitalist society has lost, but he shows also what can happen when Morris's position is popularised. With Morris, the close, personal experience of artistic creation and the awareness of the realities of work in an industrial society are usually balanced. Carpenter comes in time to divide society into two kinds of life: the ordinary, sordid, industrial work which needs to be got through, and the personal artistic creation which can go on during leisure. He works out a similar arrangement in relation to work on the land: men can be provided with small-holdings which they can work during their spare time. What happens in all these cases, with sex, art, agricultural work, is that activities taken as models of the feelings and relationships which need to become generally operative in society cease, under pressure, to be models, and become ends in themselves: the connection between the prototype and the desired actuality breaks down. If socialism is about lived experience and relationship, then there must be some means, in industrial capitalist society, of cultivating that experience, both as a measure of the quality of contemporary society and an earnest of the future: a concern with sex or art therefore becomes naturally a political involvement. But in capitalist society, these experiences will be marginal to the real business of living: the intensity of the spontaneous life of sex and art will stand out, and it is this intensity, in the general impoverishment, which makes the activities valuable. But when the step of translating this value into an actual society comes to be taken, the intensity and isolation of the activities can work against such translation. The experiences have taken on an unrelatable quality: they now seem valuable in themselves, in contrast to the mundane processes of life which characterise industrial society. Translation into real terms then sticks at the compromise that society will be a network of artists or, with Whitman, 'comrades', a linked web of individuals having deep and creative experience. The model activities become means of self-fulfilment rather than of social transformation, even if the self-fulfilment is in small communities.

There is another form of breakdown between individual spontaneous life and society, one which can be seen in a particularly acute form in Oscar Wilde's perceptive essay, *The Soul of Man Under Socialism*:

The chief advantage that would result from the establishment of Socialism is, undoubtedly, the fact that Socialism would relieve us from that sordid necessity of living for others which, in the present condition of things, presses so hardly upon almost everybody. . . .

Socialism, Communism, or whatever one chooses to call it, by converting private property into public wealth, and substituting cooperation for competition, will restore society to its proper condition of a thoroughly healthy organism, and ensure the material well-being of each member of the community. It will, in fact, give Life its proper basis and its proper environment. But, for the full development of Life to its highest mode of perfection, something more is needed. What is needed is individualism.[24]

Socialism, now, has become merely mechanism, a welcome way of arranging the business of material life and responsibility to others with the least possible trouble, so that real life, individual artistic self-expression, can be carried on without distraction. The position is the reverse of Carpenter's, but the effect in both cases is the same: Carpenter belittles the actual changes socialism involves by making it a cosmic force beyond institutions, Wilde belittles the changes by welcoming them as useful machinery for private living. Wilde makes no attempt to heal the gap between social and individual, spontaneous and socially responsible: he tries to solve the problem by accepting and ratifying the gap, turning the breakdown itself into a kind of strength. The State is to make useful products: the individual to make beautiful ones.

Wilde's position in this essay is very close to the stance taken frequently by the man who above all focuses this problem for our own time, D. H. Lawrence. If it seems impudent to bracket Lawrence with Wilde, a statement like this may clarify the similarity:

And then, when the people of the world have finally got over the state of giddy idealising of governments, nations, internations, politics, democracies, empires, and so forth; when they really understand that their collective activities are only cookhousemaid to their sheer individual activities; when they at last calmly accept a business concern for what it is; then, at last, we may actually see free men in the streets.[25]

It is the way that Lawrence places in the same category the understanding of a business concern for what it is, and an understanding that collective activities are merely the machinery for individual achievement, which captures the paradox of strength and weakness we have seen in the nineteenth century tradition. Lawrence, more than anyone, understood and fought against mechanism, emphasising in many different ways that spontaneous life must be kept free from rigid categories; but with him, too mechanism can come to mean society, as it does in the phrase 'collective activities'. The voice in this quotation is the voice of Birkin in *Women in Love*, who wants every man to have his share in the world's goods so that he can be 'rid of his importunity'. Lawrence's attitude to work is significant here:

> Work is, simply, the activity necessary for the production of a sufficient supply of food and shelter: nothing more holy than that. It is the producing of the means of self-preservation. Therefore it is obvious that it is not the be-all and end-all of existence. We work to provide means of subsistence, and when we have made provision, we proceed to live. But all work is only the making provision for what is to follow.
>
> It may be argued that work has a fuller meaning, that man lives most intensely when he works. That may be, for some few men, for some few artists whose lives are otherwise empty. But for the mass, for the 99·9 per cent of mankind, work is a form of non-living, of non-existence, of submergence. . . .[26]

The strength and weakness are again so close here that criticism is difficult, but the final judgement must surely be adverse. This is in the tradition from Arnold and Carlyle: the means of life must not be made the ends. But Lawrence's theme here is the same as Carpenter's and Wilde's: work, the merely material side of life, must be cleared out of the way so that man can perfect himself as an individual. Real living, again, is something beyond and above the actual processes of life in society: this is merely a basis. The Lawrence of *Sons and Lovers* would have recognised the falsity of this dualism which comes to pervade so much of his work: he saw there that spontaneous life in relationship is not abstractable from the living and working context in which all relationships must move, the context of the mine and the farm and the factory. When it is dislocated from this context, the intensity sets itself up against the common life, as Ursula and Skrebensky in *The Rainbow* set up the intensity of their love against 'the kaleidoscopic unreality of people', the despised routine of the city. Lawrence asks that a man should be free to be himself after work, but work itself, in a good society, should be a major part of the way a man is himself, a way of being part of a community, a relationship and not a private activity. Lawrence sees, rightly, that work in his own society has been drained of meaning, but then he ratifies this: if work is meaningless then let it be cleared away so that real living can be done. Lawrence never ceased to be committed to radical social change, but at points like this he could fail to see the value of those who were trying to return meaning to work, instead of dismissing it out of hand. He saw that change in society must come spontaneously, in the sense that no lasting change could ever be established by mechanical forcing; he saw also that the way change came was part of its meaning and value. But this sense of spontaneity lies very close to the spontaneity which resists all formulated belief out of habit, which suspects any rational and planned human creation. Lawrence exposes the problem for us in our own time, and both his strengths and weaknesses are vital to a real understanding of it.

The long tradition of criticism of industrial society in Britain which we have inherited is made primarily in terms of a sense that spontaneous living is crippled by industrial capitalism. But in recovering a sense of this spontaneous life, it has been easy to use it as the basis of an attack, not on the specific institutions of industrial capitalism but on institution itself. In one sense, this is just: any institution must stay responsive to actual, changing human needs if it is to be living, and this will mean continual renewal. What is less just is the setting up of a personal spontaneity, a personal relationship, in opposition to society itself, and envisaging the best condition as a continuing tension between the two. It was towards the fusion of spontaneous life and social responsibility that the nineteenth century tradition worked, towards the discovery of actual social institutions which could express the human freedom and fulfilment we can know now in personal relationship. The effort to preserve the full sense of spontaneous life, and yet to resist the pressure to make this merely personal, is extremely difficult; spontaneity is in one sense an invulnerable position on which to take a stand, because every other position, simply by being a formulated belief, can then be attacked as a lapse from it. It is this type of negative criticism which has to be avoided, and there are not many available prototypes of this avoidance: William Morris, who saw what the experience of art had to say about the nature of factory work, is perhaps one. Shakespeare, in the Last Comedies, could reach a kind of solution, but it is achieved within a specialised context and cannot be wholly abstracted from this. We can learn a good deal from the way Shakespeare faces his own problems, but the ultimate answer, inevitably, must be our own.

Notes to Conclusion

1. Matthew Arnold, *Poetry and Prose*, ed. John Brinson. Reynard Library, Rupert Hart-Davis, London 1954, p. 359.

2. *ibid.*, p. 365.

3. *ibid.*, 'Democracy', p. 569.

4. *ibid.*, 'Equality', p. 581.

5. Carlyle, *Signs of the Times*; Selected Works, ed. Julian Symons. Reynard Library, Rupert Hart-Davis, London 1955.

6. Carlyle, *Past and Present*. The World's Classics, Oxford University Press, 1932, p. 235.

7. *Mill on Bentham and Coleridge*, ed. F. R. Leavis. Chatto & Windus, 1962, p. 73.

8. cf. *Culture and Society* 1780-1950, by Raymond Williams. Chatto & Windus, 1958, Part 1, Ch. 3.

9. Mill, *Autobiography*. Longmans, Green and Co., 1908, pp. 38-9.

10. Mill, *On Liberty*. Basil Blackwell, Oxford, 1946 (ed. R. B. McCallum), p. 50.

11. *ibid.*, p. 52.

12. *ibid.*, p. 52.

13. Carlyle, *Chartism*. Reynard Library, p. 279.

14. *ibid.*, *Heroes and Hero-worship*, p. 324.

15. Carlyle, *Sartor Resartus*. Chapman and Hall, London 1858, p. 119.

16. Dickens, *Little Dorrit*. Oxford University Press, 1963, pp. 463-4.

17. cf. *Culture and Society*, Part 1, Ch. 5.

18. Carpenter, *Towards Democracy*. George Allen and Unwin Ltd., 1912 (pocket edition), pp. 145-6.

19. *ibid.*, pp. 44-5.

20. *ibid.*, p. 107.

21. *ibid.*, p. 73.

22. 'Democracy and the Delegate Theory', from the *Clarion*, Nov. 24th, 1894 (item in the Carpenter Collection, Central Library, Sheffield).

23. Whitman, *Democratic Vistas*. Routledge, London, 1906, p. 72f.

24. *The Works of Oscar Wilde*. Collins, 1954, pp. 1018-19.

25. D. H. Lawrence, 'Democracy', in *Pheonix*. Heinemann, 1936, p. 704.

26. *ibid.*, *Study of Thomas Hardy*, pp. 423-4.